THE ELECTION BOOK

TOM MCGUIRE was born in Longford and educated at St Mel's College, Longford and St Patrick's College, Maynooth, County Kildare. His career as a journalist began in 1990 with Radio Kerry, where he was employed as a current affairs presenter and as Head of News. In 1993 he joined RTÉ in its Cork studios where his roles included those of radio presenter, radio producer and reporter on the 'Nationwide' television programme. In 1999 he was appointed Current Affairs Editor of RTÉ Radio 1 and is currently Regional Editor of RTÉ Radio 1. He won the PPI Documentary of the Year Award in 2004 for 'The Siege of Jadotville'. Among his production credits are the 'Grassroots' series on local government and the current RTÉ Radio 1 series 'The Constituency' .

THE ELECTION BOOK

EDITED BY TOM McGUIRE

with 'The Constituencies'
by Rachael English & Nick Coffey

THE O'BRIEN PRESS
DUBLIN

First published 2007 by The O'Brien Press Ltd
12 Terenure Road East, Rathgar, Dublin 6, Ireland.
Tel: +353 1 4923333; Fax: +353 1 4922777
E-mail: books@obrien.ie
Website: www.obrien.ie

ISBN: 978-1-84717-031-6

British Library Cataloguing-in-Publication Data
The election book
1. Elections - Ireland 2. Ireland - Politics and government - 21st century
I. McGuire, Tom
324.9'417'0824

1 2 3 4 5
07 08 09 10

Editing, typesetting and design: The O'Brien Press Ltd
Printing: Creative Print and Design, Wales

Front cover image courtesy of age fotostock.

To P.M. Farrell

Acknowledgements

A project like this cannot come to fruition without a lot of goodwill, assistance, professionalism and dedication from several sources. I would like to acknowledge the attention to detail and the support the publication got from all of the staff at The O'Brien Press. Thanks also to all of the contributors to this book, for their positive and willing response, and for their generosity with their time and expertise. To all of the RTÉ staff who offered advice, assistance and experience in the course of the project. To the technical staff, particularly Tom Williams and John Doyle, without whom no edition of 'The Constituency', which provided the inspiration for the book, would ever have got to air. To my wife Ita, our family, Ciaran, Keith and Eoghan, who have listened to so much politics, they must be among the best-informed electors in any constituency!

TABLE OF CONTENTS

Introduction

From a personal point of view, I suppose you could say that general elections had an influence on me even before I was born as my parents first met during the 1948 general election campaign! Seamus McGuire and Lily Farrell were both canvassing for her brother, PM Farrell, a Clann na Poblachta candidate in Longford/Westmeath.

From the 1960s I have memories of the days when the now-derelict Esker Hall came to life as a polling booth: the painted slogans on the road; a smell of porter from the party faithful; the assisted vote for the blind; the big cars from Donegal that came to bring people to vote; and, most of all, 'the long count'.

In 1965 the long count in Longford/Westmeath took place in Longford's Temperance Hall and involved the sitting Fine Gael TD General Séan MacEoin, known as The Blacksmith of Ballinalee, and the eventual winner, Patrick Lenihan of Fianna Fáil, father of Brian Lenihan and Mary O'Rourke. While this outcome was to sever the constituency's direct link with the foundations of the State, it also heralded a great political dynasty in the midlands and beyond. It was probably one of the first times Longford featured on television, and was certainly the county's most significant public outing up to then.

It amuses me when I hear some commentators now refer to Longford/Westmeath as a 'new' constituency, when it has in fact been there since 1921, aside from a brief dalliance with Athlone in the 1930s and a recent liaison with Roscommon. The latter was a partnership that saw votes transfer within counties before parties, prompting one colourful party activist to comment that 'votes don't cross water' – the River Shannon!

Elections also evoke names and, just as sports fans recall great players and teams of the past, 'election junkies' remember the close calls, the long counts, the famous by-elections, the colourful candidates, the one-term TD and even the also-ran!

Our next-door neighbour in Killoe, County Longford, Frank Gormley, was elected to the short-lived 7th Dáil in 1932, and my father's friend, Jimmy Bennett, flew a lonesome flag for Labour in Mullingar in the 1970s when it was neither fashionable nor profitable to do so. The first election slogan I remember is that of the Independent, Joe Sheridan, in Longford/Westmeath: Vote for Joe, the Man you Know! Of course, Longford was also home to the original political slogan when, on his way to the 1st Dáil, Joseph McGuinness of Sinn Féin, who fought the 1918 election from jail, was elected on the catch-cry of 'Put him in, to get him out'.

In my journalistic career I have witnessed the drama, passion and emotion of the victors and the vanquished in the course and aftermath of elections. In 1992, in a makeshift studio in the Earl of Desmond Hotel in Tralee that served as the count-centre for Kerry North, I sat across the table from the late Tom McEllistrim when he conceded defeat. As he left the table, his place was taken by Labour party leader Dick Spring, who could only listen in awe as people like Pat Gallagher, Willie Penrose, Declan Bree and Moosajee Bhamjee, among others, were carried in on the 'Spring Tide'. The Labour party suddenly had its own 'country & western' representatives in places where some commentators didn't even think they had branches!

On my first day with RTÉ, in Cork, I remember standing at the back of City Hall during a Fianna Fáil European election convention and seeing a young, tousled-haired man in a wheelchair swept on to the ticket. Brian Crowley was to poll over 84,000 first-preference votes in that 1994 European election. Not long after that convention there were further political convulsions in the 'Beautiful City'. At a hastily convened press conference at the Imperial Hotel on the South Mall, Pat Cox TD, MEP announced his resignation from the Progressive Democrats and declared his intention to stand as an Independent in the forthcoming European election. It was a decision that was to contribute in no small way to the demise of one of the founders of the party, Desmond O'Malley, who subsequently failed to win a European seat for the PDs.

As the counting drew to a close following the general election of June 1997, another strange happening was about to occur: all twenty seats in the five Cork constituencies went to either Fianna Fáil or Fine Gael. On that weekend it seemed that the Independent and, in particular, the left-wing vote had gone down the River Lee along with Fords, Dunlops and the Verolme Cork Dockyard.

At the last general election, in 2002, my role kept me at the RTÉ Radio Centre as the marathon election results programme was broadcast. Observations here were not as personal – you cannot beat the local count-centre – but were poignant nonetheless. Who can forget the television pictures of Labour's Sean Ryan consoling a defeated Nora Owen after electronic voting had delivered the most heartless declaration in the history of the Irish electoral system? On the corridor outside the studio, in the bowels of the Radio Centre, party handlers sipped cups of tea and coffee and tried to work out the possible permutations of who would secure the last few critical seats on the final counts.

The Progressive Democrats took a justified pleasure in proving the pundits wrong and doubling the party's representation; Fine Gael's Niall Ó Muilleoir grew more ashen-faced with each passing count as yet another of his party's big-wigs bit the dust. Even in success Fianna Fáil strategist PJ Mara spoke in hushed tones when he realised Mary O'Rourke would not be part of the 29th Dáil. Nationally and locally the performance of the Independents was the real surprise of 2002, but there was no one in Dublin to speak for them!

So, what of 2007? There will be surprises and there will be changes, but from a broadcasting point of view I hope that it will be close run. Unlike the 1980s, these elections don't come around too often; punter and pundit are due some value for the vote!

The Election Book has its origins in a little radio programme that began on RTÉ Radio 1 in October 2006. In 'The Constituency', presenter Rachael English traverses the country and in the course of the series visits all of the forty-three constituencies. Her interest in politics has long been evident, particularly through her presentation of 'Five–Seven Live' and her role as an anchor, alongside Sean O'Rourke, on RTÉ Radio 1's election results programmes. It has been my privilege to produce 'The Constituency' series. By rooting the programme among the electors, the hope is that 'The Constituencies' – compiled by Rachael English and Nick Coffey and forming the second part of this book – will give the reader a particular insight into the issues, the personalities and the local idiosyncrasies which could well determine the outcome in close-run contests.

In 'The Constituencies' you will find predictions for each constituency, which are the considered opinion of the writer at a particular time and circumstance or, as the politicians are fond of saying of opinion polls, 'a snapshot in time'. The predictions will be a matter for debate and, taken in conjunction with Brian Dowling's review, will hopefully give a balanced view that can truly be 'on the one hand, or on the other hand'. In the area of forecast, I take solace from the words of Olivia O'Leary in her wonderful anthology, *Party Animals*, when she says of journalists and pundits: 'we do get it gloriously wrong, but *we* don't matter.'

The Election Book is not just about the constituencies and predictions for 2007. Throughout the year and across every Dáil term there are journalists and broadcasters who interpret events, report on matters of politics and read between the lines. This publication has provided the opportunity for familiar voices on RTÉ to commit to paper their thoughts on the electoral process; their anecdotes of other campaigns; assessments of voter intentions; expositions on electoral myths; and, for the listener or the viewer, an insight into what it is like on the other side of the microphone or camera lens.

Within the covers of this book lies an array of talent that is more often heard than read. Some, who are of a particular generation, began their journalistic careers in print and later moved to the electronic medium; others have joined the ranks quite recently. They all share a passion for politics. From a professional point of view, the depth of reflection on the subject matter is clear. This collection of commentaries allows the reader to track the evolution of election coverage in our democracy, to explore the efficacy of opinion polls, to compare and contrast the benefits, or otherwise, of an electronic vote against a paper ballot and to reflect on the influence of the Irish vote in the USA in the nineteenth century, or of the ballot from Mountjoy Prison in the twenty-first century. There is place, too, for the characters from across the last four decades: from the church-gate meetings of the 1960s through to the arrival of the computer age, there are anecdotes and tales from the campaign trail and about the varied denizens and colourful representatives who have peopled the Dáil and the Seanad down through the years.

On St Valentine's Day 1997 Kerry county councillor Jackie Healy-Rae met Bertie Ahern in Leinster House in an effort to persuade the Fianna Fáil party to run three candidates in the upcoming general election. It was a journey in vain, but the start of another odyssey for the Independent from Kerry South. I was in Scott's Hotel, Killarney, almost two months later when Councillor Healy-Rae announced his departure from Fianna Fáil, and launched what turned out to be a successful campaign to secure a Dáil seat in the constituency. Firing a warning shot across the bows to Bertie Ahern and Fianna Fáil, Healy-Rae said he would win a seat and that 'they'll dance to my music before this is all over'.

In 2007 the band has already started playing, the courtships have begun and very soon now the fat lady will sing!

Tom McGuire

I. Reminiscences of an on-the-run Psephologist

John Bowman

The interest of voters in quickly learning the national trend of election results is at least as old as broadcasting itself. But it was London restaurants and department stores which first attempted to meet this demand. In November 1922 *The Times* detailed the elaborate arrangements that had been made 'to enable the great crowds which will flock to the West-end of London tonight' to learn the election results 'in comfort and without delay'. Individual counts and the state of the parties would be displayed at some major stores, while in Trafalgar Square there would be 'a band and cinematograph performance' to entertain the crowds in the intervals between announcements.

The aim was to ensure that election night 'should be a great festival for London', with leading restaurants displaying the positions of the parties, as well as the fate of individual politicians, 'within a few minutes of the results being known at the polling stations'. Selfridges even promised the innovation that at regular intervals it would send up 'coloured lights showing which party is leading at the polls'. The colours chosen were red for the Liberals, blue for the Conservatives, green for Labour and amber for the National Liberals.[1] Peter Snow would, I hope, have been impressed.

Similar arrangements were in place in October 1924. Indeed, such was the excitement in London on this election night that

1   *The Times*, 15 November 1922.

several citizens were charged before the Bow Street magistrates the following day, including an 'infirm old man with a white beard' who was alleged to have been disorderly near the Houses of Parliament. His excuse to the court was that he had become 'excited when he heard some men discussing Bolshevism, and he was having a fight with one of them when the police intervened'.[2]

My own introduction to election results fever – if that is the appropriate term – was the installation of what looked like a giant cricket scoreboard on the *Irish Times'* building in Westmoreland Street, in Dublin, which displayed the state of the parties during the 1957 election. This I could read from the top of the No. 10 bus on my way to school, and it was more up-to-date than that morning's newspaper. Taking note of the party tallies at 9.00am, I could then update the figures when passing by again in mid-afternoon, by which time further seats had been added to the official results. It could be as exciting or as tame as a five-day cricket match. Radio Éireann, as it then was, did not compete. At that time it did not even broadcast during mid-morning or mid-afternoon, still less get involved in the public service of being first with the most significant news in any democracy at election time: who governs next?

The politicians, too, as the historical record shows, were reticent when it came to broadcasting. From the very beginning their instinct was 'to steer clear, as far as possible, of politics and religion'.[3] In 1932 a modest proposal was put to the Broadcasting Advisory Committee suggesting that some 'short speeches or statements by representatives of the various political parties'

2   *The Times*, 31 October 1924.

3   JJ Walsh, Minister for Posts and Telegraphs to PS O'Hegarty, secretary, Posts and Telegraphs, 21 May 1926, RTÉ Written Archives.

should be broadcast during the general election campaign. This was duly submitted to the Cumann na nGaedheal government, but with a recommendation that it be rejected. The government was reminded that when the radio service was launched, it had been decided 'to debar the broadcasting of all matter of a controversial political character'. It was desirable to continue with such a policy 'in view of the impracticability of exercising any control over the actual matter which might be broadcast, and the abuse which might ensue if unrestricted political broadcasts were permitted.' Finance minister Ernest Blythe scarcely needed such discouragement. His own policy was expressed in his decision on the file: 'I am against political broadcasting.'[4]

Before the 1937 election a proposal came from Radio Éireann's director, TJ Kiernan, that the station might broadcast contributions from the political parties. He instanced the 'successful innovation' of the Budget broadcasts of 1935 and 1936, adding that the speakers had been 'microphoned into cautiousness'. He allowed that the election environment was 'somewhat different and more difficult'. His own preference was for a half-hour debate between candidates nominated by the parties:

> 'This would have to be an impromptu broadcast and is obviously dangerous, but if a good chairman, outside party politics, were found, I think it is an experiment worth trying.'

Kiernan's preference was for each politician to speak for five minutes, followed by ten minutes of questioning by the Chair and a

---

4   O'Hegarty, 4 February 1932, Posts and Telegraphs file in RTÉ Written Archives.

five-minute summary by the Chair, who might, he suggested, be Edmund Curtis, then Professor of Irish History at Trinity College, Dublin. In all, the proposal commended itself to Kiernan as 'a democratic use of the radio for political purposes'.[5] This was received with caution, the minister being reminded by his department secretary that 'the proposal now made is obviously full of dangers in an inflammatory atmosphere such as ours'.[6]

In 1948 there was again a clamour for broadcasting opportunities during the winter election, with much emphasis being placed on the dangers to the health of the public should they attend political meetings in what was one of the worst winters in living memory. The incumbents – Fianna Fáil – were again hostile to the idea, probably on the grounds that the vitriol of the attacks, especially from Seán MacBride's Clann na Poblachta, should not be granted air-time.[7] Quidnunc, writing in 'An Irishman's Diary' column in *The Irish Times*, was one among many who called for Radio Éireann to provide electioneering opportunities to the parties. He surmised that the broadcaster's timidity on the matter could be put down to a concern that it could only lead to 'endless trouble'.[8] The radio critic of the *Evening Herald* believed the politicians were also shy of radio:

---

5   Kiernan to Oscar Traynor, Minister for Posts and Telegraphs, 16 March 1937 in Posts and
     Telegraphs file, 'Broadcasting proposals in connection with forthcoming General
     Elections: proposals rejected', RTÉ Written Archives.

6   O'Hegarty to Traynor, 10 April 1937, *ibid*. O'Hegarty was no stranger to inflammatory
     communication himself: in his *A history of Ireland under the Union: 1801-1922* (London, 1952)
     an index entry under de Valera reads: 'his vain and foolish mission to America', p.793.

7   See *Evening Mail*, 17 January 1948.

8   The *Irish Times*, 9 February 1948.

'Radio is sincere, and without sincerity at the mike there will be no truth trickling through the receiver set. It is, in short, the domestic lie-detector, and, as such, may well be passed up by the politicians in favour of the open-air forum.'[9]

Meanwhile Radio Éireann did promise that its final programme of the evening, the sponsored Hospitals Trusts programme, would include live news of any results that became available during the broadcast. Independent Newspapers were more ambitious. They promised that the election of each member of the new Dáil would be announced on an electric news sign on a city-centre building rented for the occasion:

'The results would also be broadcast by a public address system from the same building, the announcer being the well-known radio commentator, Mr Eamonn Andrews. In the intervals, items of election news from the various centres of counting will be given to the public.'

There would also be 'a programme of gramophone records'. It was no coincidence that the rented building was close to the headquarters of its rival title, the *Irish Press*, on Burgh Quay.[10]

During the elections of the 1950s there was some solution provided to the dearth of election coverage by the introduction of a series of party political broadcasts, which facilitated the advocacy of partisan viewpoints without Radio Éireann itself becoming

9   OG Dowling, 'Air Space for politicians?', *Evening Herald*, 15 January 1948.

10   *Irish Independent*, 5 February 1948.

embroiled in controversy. The broadcasters seemed content to act merely as facilitators, timekeepers and publishers.

That Radio Éireann might have some further duty on results night was reflected in Comhairle Radio Éireann's minutes and the suggestion that 'if feasible, the Station should be kept open late, as occasion required, to announce results'.[11] At the following election the Comhairle 'congratulated the News Room and the Announcing Staff on the effective manner in which the Election Results were broadcast.'[12] Alas, no trace of these has survived in RTÉ's Sound Archive.

In general it can be confidently asserted that radio current affairs was very tardy in accepting its opportunities and responsibilities. Indeed, it waited until television had carved out a new frontier for current affairs in the early 1960s before taking its own early steps. So reticent was it prior to television's arrival that, insofar as current affairs was concerned, this could justly be described as the golden age of *silent* radio.

It was not until the election of 1965 that RTÉ engaged in its first serious attempt at results coverage on radio and television. Garret FitzGerald played such a starring role on television – advising on the shape of the programme as well as participating in it – that it proved a considerable advantage in his imminent senate campaign, which launched his political career.[13] Some fragments of the 1965 radio coverage have survived in RTÉ's Sound Archive. At one stage, during the count, anchor Kevin O'Kelly asked one of those

11   Minutes Comhairle Radio Éireann, 6 March 1954.

12   Minutes Comhairle Radio Éireann, 9 March 1957.

13   Garret FitzGerald, *All in a life; an autobiography* (Dublin, 1991), pp.69-70.

manning the analysis desk, Brian Farrell, for a prediction of what the party totals might be in the incoming Dáil. Farrell replied:

> 'My own belief is that, at this stage, to start estimating or guesstimating or simply hunching what those will be is a waste of time. I mean, we will know it within twenty-four hours and we will know it on the basis of what the people have said and, so far, what the people have said from constituency to constituency has varied quite an amount. I don't think there's an easy regular pattern to be established.'

Fellow political scientist and broadcaster David Thornley must have raised an eyebrow at this reply because Farrell added: 'David, do you think this is being just too cagey for words?' Thornley rejoined:

> 'I think you *are* just being too cagey for words, Brian. To be quite honest, I agree that you can't predict this thing with any confidence. But after all that's what we're here for; to stick our necks out – at least that's one of the things we're here for – and on the basis of expert knowledge which we are supposed to possess, to fall flat on our faces for the general delectation of the listener and this I am prepared to do, for one.' [14]

In fairness, this was before the explosion in expert studies on Irish politics and elections – many of them written by Farrell, Thornley and their pupils – and long before the term 'psephology'

---

14   1965 General Election, results programme, RTÉ Sound Archive.

came to be at all understood in Irish political circles. And Thornley well knew that what the public best remembered were predictions where the forecasters *did* fall flat on their faces.

Psephology is indeed an arcane discipline. It is defined as the study of elections, electoral behaviour and voting trends that help predict election results. The word is of relatively recent origin, having been coined about half-a-century ago as an academic jest from *psephos*, the Greek word for pebble. In an era before electronic voting, or hanging chads, or even our traditional pencil and paper, the Ancient Greeks expressed their preferences for a particular candidate by dropping pebbles into urns.[15]

Perhaps we need a different word to describe the challenge of election-night broadcasting, when one is practising what might be called on-the-run psephology: attempting to forecast a constituency outcome while successive counts are becoming available. This is a high-wire act, especially as one is dealing with so many other challenges during the course of such a broadcast.

Most psephology is practised in much calmer surroundings, invariably when each count has been tabulated and the election result is already known. It is much easier to explain *why* a constituency voted as it did when you know *how* it voted. On a live broadcast one is attempting the why and how questions at a moment when both are unknowns.

If it is hazardous, it is also somewhat thankless. Listeners and viewers — and especially politicians — invariably remember any wrong calls, especially pessimistic ones. And sometimes they even complain about quite valid observations. Commenting on the 1981

15   The word was coined by RB McCallum, sometime Master of Pembroke College, Oxford and co-author of the first of the celebrated Nuffield studies of British General Elections, RB McCallum and Alison Readman, *British General Election of 1945* (Oxford, 1947). See also, Austin Ranney, 'Thirty Years of "Psephology"', *British Journal of Political Science*, Vol. 6, No. 2 (Apr., 1976), pp. 217-230.

election results, James Tully, the Labour deputy from Meath, complained to the RTÉ Director-General that 'your commentators were so ready to write-off so many people, including myself, without getting the facts of the case. It was rather annoying to those who were not at the count, but who were vitally interested in the result to be told that the people are in trouble when in fact this has no relation whatever to the fact.'

Tully added modestly that 'perhaps this small matter might be considered at any future election.'[16] This was rather self-serving as Tully's seat was indeed at some risk from the first count, in which his Labour running-mate, Frank McLaughlin, had surprised him by out-polling him on first preferences. The Labour seat was never in doubt, but who would win it was. It was only Tully's marginally better performance on transfers that saved him.

Another complainant was Clem Coughlan, who was concerned that 'hardly any mention at all' was given to his constituency of Donegal South West, which, he claimed, had shown 'a better performance from Fianna Fáil's point of view than any other constituency in the country'. In fact, it had turned in quite an average performance and in as many as nineteen other constituencies Fianna Fáil had done better.[17]

Gratuitous criticism is another hazard. In the course of a recent survey of the national hurling championship, Keith Duggan in the sports pages of *The Irish Times* allowed himself this swipe at the author: 'The championship is such an epic affair now. It starts out

16   James Tully to Waters, 22 June 1981, RTÉ Written Archives.

17   Clem Coughlan to Waters, 23 June 1981, RTÉ Written Archives. Donegal South West was within 0.1 per cent of Fianna Fáil's national average. Coughlan was on surer ground when he added that 'the ordinary country folk would like to have seen their own particular areas given more mention. We were inundated with the views of a few selected TDs from the Dublin area, some of whose performances were not that brilliant. Ireland seems to start and finish in Dublin and the rest of us are just a few statistics thrown in to make a total.'

much like one of those marathon election night television sessions, when John Bowman confronts the nation with a solemn face and absurd tie and lets the country know that it's going to be a long time before he can make sense of anything.'[18]

I did not recognise this picture as I have always believed that it is the broadcaster's duty in a results programme to continuously attempt to predict the outcome by making sense of every available clue – latest tallies, early results, constituency intelligence, probable transfer patterns, the evidence of the exit poll – all laced with a dollop of intuition. So, prompted in part by Duggan's criticism, I re-examined my opening remarks in the 2002 election to see whether I had said anything resembling his recollection. In the opening minute of the programme, with only seventeen seats filled, I offered the following prediction: 'a good election for Fianna Fáil; very poor for Fine Gael – possibly losses of twenty seats; modest gains for Labour; and solid gains for the Progressive Democrats, Sinn Féin, the Greens and Independents.' The bit that was best remembered of this prediction was 'modest gains for Labour': they didn't happen, any gains being offset by as many losses. But Fianna Fáil did gain four seats, Fine Gael lost twenty-three, the Progressive Democrats, Sinn Féin and the Greens all gained four and the Independents gained seven. I took as much umbrage from his comments on my tie: it is thirty years old, made by my wife and I am so fond of it that I wear it on every election broadcast.

Election results night is a moment of truth for the entire country. The collective voice of the Irish voter has spoken on Election Day and on the following day – or, sometimes, days – that voice is heard. It is an awesome moment in any democracy. And

18   Keith Duggan, 'A riveting story of hurling's golden era', *The Irish Times*, 12 November 2005.

for as long as we are without electronic voting machines, it will remain a slow moment. In any cost–benefit analysis of the two systems, I believe that among the benefits of the manual voting system should be the fact that for many younger citizens their first engagement with democracy is often kindled by the excitement generated by RTÉ's results coverage. It is also becoming acknowledged among academics that the communal involvement of the electorate during election night results programming is a significant event in a democracy.[19]

Since the 1970s Irish elections have been passing through by far their most volatile period since Independence. Moreover, many of the election results have been indecisive, presenting multiple choices to the two leaders who would be Taoiseach. In consequence, some of the post-election jockeying for position has begun in the election results studio. Indeed, I think it could be fairly claimed that Irish elections in recent decades have been among the most exciting anywhere in the democratic world. Where British election counts could be likened to six hundred games of draughts – with the outcome in two-thirds of them foregone conclusions – attempting to read the outcome in the constituencies which emerge as marginal during an Irish election can be akin to playing multiple chess matches simultaneously. As one revisits a constituency after each count, some fresh conundrum may present.

One other point needs to be borne in mind. Politicians from long-established western democracies are regularly invited to act as international observers in emerging democracies in Africa or

---

19   See the comparative study of election night television coverage in 1968 and 2000 in Thomas E. Patterson, *Diminishing Returns*, (Kennedy School of Government, Harvard, 2003).

Eastern Europe in order to validate the election procedures and to declare whether they meet criteria of being free and fair. They witness millions of voters queuing to mark voting papers and putting them into boxes, later to be counted manually. Of what value would their scrutiny be in an electronic system? At least if an election is conducted fraudulently in a paper-based system, the cheating political faction has to use the army or a number of party workers to effect the fraud, therefore the corruption can never be a secret among some elite cabal. This need not be the case with an electronic voting system, however, where a small group of programmers could deliver any dictator's requirements.

The conventional wisdom in recent years is that the marathon election counts may soon be a thing of the past. If electronic voting is introduced in Ireland, it will be possible to pull a lever and show the final result in a matter of minutes once the computers have spoken. But there are many matters in life where we do not take this utilitarian approach. We solemnise some events, such as marriages, funerals, presidential inaugurations, school prizegivings and many others, with rituals that oblige us to take time and give due recognition to an important moment.

Is there not a strong case to be made that we should equally pay homage to the ritual of having one's vote counted – and to the important Irish variant of seeking to give that vote expression in later counts? Does this not deserve the nation's attention for twenty-four hours while the larger question at the heart of every election is in the balance: who governs next?

The Progressive Democrats recently voted at their annual conference to abandon electronic voting. Michael McDowell has admitted that he is not 'mad keen' on it and has a personal preference for paper ballots: 'I regard the paper system as having a lot of merit. People trust it and understand it, and watching extended counts on television is educational. These are all merits that shouldn't be forgotten.'[20]

It is especially the case that the electorate is very open – admittedly, I base this largely on anecdotal feedback from listeners and viewers – to learning more about the complexities of proportional representation (PR). It often strikes me that this is akin to that fraction of the television viewership of snooker, tennis or showjumping who appreciate the excitement of the competition without knowing all the complexities of the scoring systems.[21] Many voters who well understand the method of *voting* are not fully aware of the method of *counting* in a multi-seat PR election. And it is the broadcasting of the results over many hours which has introduced vast numbers of them to how this can matter. This in turn better informs their voting strategy in future elections.

Among the many letters of congratulations to the then Director-General of RTÉ George Waters after the 1981 results coverage was one from the newly elected Fine Gael TD, Mary Flaherty. She suggested that 'interest in and information about the PR system must now be at its highest even in Ireland and in no small measure due to RTÉ.'[22]

If that accolade was deserved – and I believe it was – one man more than any other should take a considerable amount of the credit. This was the late High Court judge Sean O'Leary, who in the general election results programmes of the 1980s set a new

20   *The Irish Times*, 29 April 2006.

21   I met countless viewers who were enthusing about the television coverage of the 2006 Ryder Cup, only a fraction of whom knew the difference between a four-ball contest and a foursome.

22   Mary Flaherty to George T. Waters, 26 June 1981, RTÉ Written Archives.

standard in what anchors might expect from party spokespersons. Having been influential – as Fine Gael's director of elections – in determining strategy in each constituency, O'Leary left his party hat outside the studio door once the results programme went on the air and offered disinterested evaluations of who might win the seats once he saw the first-count figures. Where other party spokespersons kept HQ happy by falling back on the formula – 'I think we'll hang in there and shade it at the finish' – O'Leary was quite prepared to admit when a Fine Gael candidate was in trouble. Factors related to statistics, geography, gender, ideology, inter-candidate rivalry and any other factor peculiar to the constituency were brought into play in his forecasts.

He could also be forthright in his dismissal of pretenders. Election broadcasts – as is attested in RTÉ's archives – are laced with some pretty ropey commentary by those who don't know their limitations. On one occasion, when anchoring the radio coverage of the 1981–82 elections, I asked a constituency reporter how the party tallymen at the count-centre were reading the destination of the final seat. Instead of answering truthfully that he did not know because he had not sounded them on the matter, he gambled bravely by offering his own forecast of how each count would turn out. We all could have been taken out of our misery had some hard result become available from elsewhere and interrupted his exposition. Instead, his sally occurred during a lull in proceedings and there was ample time for our hapless reporter to elaborate – and with each prediction he became more and more implausible.

While I wondered how I would euphemistically throw in some health warning at the conclusion, I got a signal from O'Leary that he wanted to offer a verdict:

'In the course of many years listening to election coverage I've had to listen to a fair amount of *raimeis*, but that beats them all. Total codswallop.'

John Bowman joined RTÉ in 1962. He has covered general elections and analysed political developments for many years on both radio and television. He has chaired the audience-participation political programme 'Questions and Answers' since 1998 and he presents 'Bowman: Sunday Morning' on RTÉ Radio 1. Author of *De Valera and the Ulster Question 1917–1973*.

II. Voting early and often

Tom McGurk

Curiously, I received the most illustrative window into the Irish and electoral politics when some years ago I was making a television documentary series entitled 'Long Journey Home – The History of Irish America'. Much of our research was done on the political machine of the Boston Irish and it provided a fascinating glimpse into the beginnings of an enthusiasm and a fascination with the electoral process that survives here in Ireland to this day. What was painted large in this research was that the Famine Irish, and the thousands more who arrived subsequently, took very little to America apart from their desperate needs and an understanding of the democratic process.

Seemingly, no sooner had they stepped off the boat than they were introduced to what famously became known in America as 'Ward-boss politics'. Frequently it was even a local Irish-Bostonian politician who might meet them off the boat, sort their accommodation out and perhaps even a job – and they were his voters for generations afterwards. Thus began for many what was to become a generational relationship with the political system, which from the outset was intimate, tribal and instinctive.

Whereas other emigrants headed westwards, the Irish remained in the big cities. Perhaps post-Famine they would never again put their trust in fields and crops. As a result, the Famine Irish into America were the first to establish what became known as the ghetto – impoverished areas in the large cities – where the Irish congregated in huge numbers; virtually recreating the village atmosphere from back home.

They huddled together for protection and for solace (the last anti-Catholic riot in Boston, which resulted in a convent being burned down, had occurred as recently as 1863), and they used the extended family as the basic unit of this society; at its centre was the priest and the politician. Apart from hard work, politics became the instrument of their economic and social liberation. Instinctively where they felt this had been stymied back at home, America offered not only the prospect of a new life but also a new politics.

These miniature 'Irelands' in America survived late into the nineteenth century, until the Irish began to join the lower middle-class to become what was famously known later as the 'lace-curtain Irish'. This ghetto living was not unique to the Irish – the Italians and the Jews were to follow suit – but what became unique about the Irish end of town was its organisation and determination about politics.

It was in their blood, of course. Daniel O'Connell's Repeal Movement had revolutionised Irish peasant political knowledge and from the beginning these new arrivals in America saw the political system there as the beginning of their journey to their new lives in the new world. Importantly, they had an immense faith in the power of political organisation to transform their circumstances and a fundamental understanding of how the American Constitution allowed for this.

Important as all this was for the Irish, it also became a defining moment in American political life. The mass politics the Irish introduced in the middle of the nineteenth century was an important precedent. Given the power of this type of tribal politics, it is no wonder that a century later Tip O'Neill, former

Speaker of the House, could famously comment that 'all politics are essentially local'.

The elite Brahmins of Boston were initially amazed and alarmed by this turn of events. Suddenly, for the first time, patronage and oligarchy in politics were being threatened by numbers. Even though the franchise was still not widely universal at the time, in nineteenth-century America voting and political involvement were regarded as essentially the privilege of the wealthy and the educated. No wonder, then, that the constant Yankee complaint about the new Irish was that they were 'too fond of drink and politics'.

The notion that 'poor Paddy' – probably illiterate and speaking little English and with his voting slip in his hand – was the democratic equal of the wealthy white Anglo-Saxon Protestants, who constituted the elite of this new nation, came as a huge shock to the American body-politic. Yet within a generation these Irish paupers had transformed the American political system into a competition of mass franchise and with it, too, both the newly emerging Democratic party and the first trade unions. Importantly, for the first time the concerns of the very poor, the conditions and the circumstances under which they existed, became part of political discourse.

Interestingly, the units of the American democratic system, designed as it was on small local franchises culminating in larger and larger territories, was uniquely suited to the Irish approach. For the Irish, once you got hold of the ward, you took City Hall and, beyond that, House and Senate seats. Thus the 'city ward', the smallest American political unit of the electorate, became the cockpit of this new democratic revolution. As its centre the Irish installed the 'Ward-boss' – the political fixer who controlled this emerging political machine. He knew everybody and everything about them, he turned up at all the wakes and weddings and, most importantly of all, he solved problems.

Essentially the Ward-boss was responding to what these early electoral pioneers understood politics to be about, practical things such as jobs, houses, wages, sewage, schools and the police force. Whereas before their arrival politics had been the exclusive hobby of the educated and wealthy pioneering American elite, the Famine Irish saw it as a mass movement, a fundamental instrument of social and economic architecture. Released from their colonial bondage back home, where their political representation was stymied within the imperial templates of the age, they realised that politics in their new land was potentially a journey of indefinite promise.

To understand current Irish political architecture, a closer examination of the nineteenth-century Irish-American Ward-boss is instructive. Importantly, not only did he run a political system but he was also a 'fixer', an organiser and a patron: jobs, houses, health, education, legal, even loans and practical help were the lot of the Ward-boss. This system established the direct relationship between politics and economic and social concerns; politics was about fixing things, solving problems, helping out.

Consequently a whole new currency of political measurement emerged: you voted for those who helped you and your family when in need. Naturally this scenario is familiar to us now, but in nineteenth-century America, political life before the arrival of the Irish had been a rich-man's hobby, a discourse conducted among an elite few, out of sight and hearing of the many. The notion of the politician as a 'fixer' superseded, for the first time, the notion of the politician as a dilettante of ideas.

The other major influence on this emerging political approach was the fact that in the emigrant Irish community at the time, the extended family was the cornerstone of society. This generated cohesion and tribal loyalty and, significantly, the notion of the 'political family'. Whereas in American politics the Kennedys are a prototype, we can barely imagine the domestic Irish political scene without the prevalence of family. As the Ward-boss went about his daily business, knowing everyone and their relatives, checking the living and the dead and getting the tribe out on polling day, he was initiating in America a way of politics that has survived in Ireland to this day.

Political activity also quickly became a community activity, and the democratic exercise became the muscle-flexing of the new Irish arrivals. Importantly, too, was that from O'Connell's Ireland they brought with them the tradition of public politics, or politics as spectacle, thus their legacy to America also includes the marching band, the bonfire and the monster meeting. Indeed, much of the razzmatazz of contemporary American politics owed its origins to the emigrant Irish who took its flavours with them. Election day was run out of the bars and the shebeens – what's changed? It was a party, a *céilí* and presumably it all ended up with sore heads the following day.

Then of course the Boston research we worked through was hugely familiar in that there were endless complaints from the Yankee establishment about impersonation and all sorts of 'Irish political dirty tricks'. Yes, it seems the dead were up and voting, early and often too, in nineteenth-century Boston, New York and Philadelphia. Much of this came to a head with the election of the famous James Michael Curley, the first ever Irish Catholic Mayor of Boston. In retrospect, Curley's controversial life now seems in some ways emblematic of so much of the recent controversy in Irish political life.

Despised as a 'fixer' and accused of corruption, Curley was loved and hated with equal passion. His Tammany Hall politics later became a by-word for political corruption but, as Curley himself always insisted, the poor ghetto Irish did not enjoy the many secret societies of their wealthy opponents whereby the corruption of the privileged was invisible. On one occasion, after numerous complaints about impersonation – i.e. the difficulty of telling just how many Murphys and O'Tooles and McGuires there actually were – Curley's opponents decided to introduce photo identity. Curley was accused of responding by getting the thousands of Chinese in Boston to vote for him because nobody could tell one from the other.

Apart from the roguery, Curley was important because he was the weapon employed by mass franchise politics to make things happen. If your son wanted to join the police force or the fire department, you went to see the Mayor. When it snowed in Boston, Curley had thousands of brushes stored in the basement of City Hall to instantly hand out to the unemployed to give them a few days' work clearing the snow. As other Irish people rose to prominence in the trade unions and the education and alcohol trades, Curley was faced with accusations that now the Irish had a 'political mafia'. A generation on, then, the Irish had come a long way from the coffin-ships and the key to that progress was not economic, it was political.

The Boston research proved hugely evocative of the instinctive and primeval passions about politics that survive to this day, with its songs, poems and tunes about political life, and the wonderful and colourful election posters. (I remember once, on a general election campaign in the west of Ireland, watching Charles Haughey being welcomed to small towns in east Galway by a line of men carrying burning sods of turf on pitch forks. One man I asked about it told me that the tradition had begun in the days of Charles Stuart Parnell.)

I think for the Irish, both at home and abroad, this passion for politics has been a direct historical legacy of the colonial era. The passion for freedom and political sovereignty was, in the first instance, a political battle, but what lay behind all this was their lives and their standards of living. For the American-Irish in particular, who had, after all, survived the catastrophe that was the Great Famine, it was born out of the memories of the years of terrible suffering and deprivation that only began to end with their arrival in America. No wonder they saw politics as somehow akin to a life and death struggle – it had literally been that for so many of them.

No wonder, too, that Irish-American writer Pete Hamill recalled, many years afterwards, his utter confusion at the floods of tears he saw flowing down his father's face when, as a child in 1960, he stood on a street corner in New York with his father to watch Senator John Fitzgerald Kennedy, who was on the campaign trail for the US Presidency. Kennedy went past, Hamill recalls, like 'some bronzed God'. Perhaps it is instructive to wonder just why Hamill's father was crying. Was he crying for the millionaire son of a billionaire Irish-American family now long removed from the ghetto in which the Hamills still lived? Or was he crying for the lost generations of the miles walked, the doors knocked and the lists checked? Was he, in fact, crying to witness the ghostly generational army of fixers and talliers and Ward-bosses finally achieve all that hope and determination had led them for fight for, so hard and so long?

THE ELECTION BOOK

Tom McGurk began broadcasting with RTÉ Radio in 1972 and television in 1974. Currently anchoring sports television and radio talk and current affairs programmes on RTÉ, his principal work has been in the area of drama and television documentary. He writes a column for the *Sunday Business Post* and is currently writing a Ph.D. thesis on Samuel Beckett.

III. E-voting: dead or alive?

Sean O'Rourke

It happened so long ago now that the pain has eased, but my despondency at the news was total. They're what? Changing the voting system? Going electronic? Yes, and what's more we'll have all the results a couple of hours after the close of poll, thanks to a computer system that can crunch the numbers within minutes. What, one wondered, about the great traditions of Irish elections, the long counts, the tallies, the pencil chewing, the suspense, shocks, passion, drama and, above all, the sorcery of the experts like Michael Gallagher or the late Judge Sean O'Leary, who could look six counts ahead in ten constituencies and predict the overall outcome?

This change, I was convinced, was about as welcome as the notion of telling fiddlers they were no longer needed at the national Fleadh Cheoil because we now have synthesisers that can play automatically. There would be music in the streets alright, but would it inspire a young man to pick up an instrument and start to play it himself? Would the crowds turn up? General elections, and the way we have followed the results, are as much a part of Irish culture and public entertainment as the Galway races, the Munster Hurling Final and a vital Triple Crown match – all rolled into one festival of competitiveness. What other event offers the same audience participation and the occasional chance for the little guy to come from nowhere and put one over on the big players?

My own love affair with elections was cemented thirty years ago, on the last day of my university exams, the day the boxes were opened in Election '77. I have no memory of the exam subject, but can remember well being glued to the television coverage from the moment Brian Farrell, trademark rose in his lapel, opened the show.

All the pundits had predicted victory for the outgoing Fine Gael–Labour coalition. Their position had been fireproofed, it appeared, by a clever constituency revision. It was designed to ensure government candidates would win two out of three seats where they were stronger, and take two seats in the four-seaters, where Fianna Fáil had the edge. There was a small radio perched on the arm of the couch for use during the television advertisements, and I can still hear Tim Pat Coogan enthusing in the early hours of the following morning about how the big headline in the *Irish Press* would run: It Could be Over 80.

In fact, this was an underestimate of the Fianna Fáil seat count, which turned out to be an astonishing eighty-four seats in the greatest landslide of modern Irish politics. 'Jack Is Back' would be the *Irish Independent*'s headline over the story of Fianna Fáil's return to single-party government with a twenty-seat majority. The constituency revision had turned out to be too clever by half as Fianna Fáil took two seats in most of the three-seaters and three out of four in some of the four-seat constituencies.

The previous Sunday the political correspondents, to a man, had predicted the return of Cosgrave's Fine Gael–Labour government. Sean Duignan memorably observed that a win for Fianna Fáil would be 'the biggest comeback since Lazarus'. A week later they were invited back to eat crow as presenter Kevin Healy replayed their words, noting that not only had Lazarus come back but he'd brought some of his friends along, too.

Although I can vaguely recall seeing a learned man with the unusual name of Basil Chubb on black-and-white television in the 1960s, the aforementioned love of election coverage really began in

1973. When my class was supposedly preparing for the Leaving Certificate, a bunch of us started hanging out in the Fine Gael headquarters beside the bookie's office, down the street from our school in Galway. There we learned about the nuts and bolts of campaigning, and there was palpable excitement at the prospect of a change of government after sixteen years of unbroken Fianna Fáil rule. On Election Day itself, there was shock and awe when one of the lads announced that he had actually voted – unusual for a seventeen-year-old when the voting age was twenty-one.

The big star of the count was Ted Nealon, then with RTÉ Current Affairs, whose intimate knowledge of the constituencies led him early on to predict victory for the National Coalition being offered by Liam Cosgrave and Brendan Corish on the basis of a fourteen-point plan aimed primarily at bringing down the cost of living.

In defeat, Fianna Fáil leader Jack Lynch gamely suggested that he was handing over the country in good shape and would like it back in the same condition. Brian Lenihan accepted the loss of his seat in Roscommon–Leitrim like a man. Such moments linger in the memory, as does the deadpan response of Labour leader Frank Cluskey to an aggressive question about why he lost his seat in 1981: 'I didn't get enough votes.'

Like no other, elections are the People's Day. As the ultimate deciders, their power at the ballot box is absolute and when the mood is angry it can be as awesome to watch as the sea in a storm. What scriptwriter in 1992 would have given us Moosajee Bhamjee's election in County Clare; fourteen seats for a party not two years in existence, as happened with the Progressive Democrats in 1987; or, indeed, the loss of 60 per cent of that party's ten seats a decade later?

The point of recalling all this is to emphasise just how much the way in which the ordinary voter has been able to follow elections is a vital part of our democratic culture. Election counts are events that capture the imagination and can inspire people to become involved in politics. They should not be changed without compelling reasons.

So it was with very mixed emotions that I began preparing, in early 2002, to anchor RTÉ Radio 1's General Election results programme for the second time. It is an awesome privilege, and one given to very few broadcasters, but my enthusiasm was tempered with regret. In all likelihood, it would be the last time a current affairs presenter, surrounded by all manner of partial and impartial expert analysts, would call in reporters and participants from every constituency in the land to hear of tally figures, expectations, predictions, agonies, ecstasies and, at the end of the day, the facts and figures.

For all its marvels and advantages, and its ability to bring voters visually into the drama of the moment, television, in its cumbersome way, has never matched radio's speed in reacting to a breaking story. It will usually have live cameras at only half the count-centres, whereas radio is everywhere at all times. For some reason, radio manages to be that little bit ahead with analysis and results, or so the *cognoscenti* will usually tell you.

In 2002 there was the excitement of a new element to the proceedings, courtesy of e-voting, with three constituencies yielding final results on election night itself, ahead of the usual seventeen-hour marathon on the main count day. When it was all over, it seemed inevitable that e-voting would be used everywhere next time round. With a nonchalance that even to this day I find breathtaking, government ministers acknowledged that it would mean less of an engagement by the public with the whole process, and that a lot of excitement would go out of the count once the results could be processed rapidly. Why did they not care about this?

Equally puzzling was the fact that no one on the opposition benches shouted STOP! when trite arguments about the old system being silly and outdated were put forward. Perhaps the general enthusiasm for e-voting, at the initial stages, can be traced to the agonies inflicted by the old counting system on exhausted candidates of all shades. Anything to get it over with, seemed to be the unspoken verdict of the practitioners. And so, in the absence of any public demand and with virtually no debate, e-voting went ahead and was deemed a success. The biggest lesson was that candidates should hear the results privately, prior to public declaration, to avoid the cruelty and humiliation endured by Fine Gael TD Nora Owen, whose defeat came as news to her at the same time as it did to the country at large.

Were it not for the doggedness of some citizens, who had concerns about the safety of the system, we would now be facing into a general election in which e-voting was employed in every constituency. Instead, their misgivings eventually persuaded the opposition, and then the government, that it would be unwise to embrace the new system without being absolutely certain that it was both reliable and tamper-proof.

Unfortunately for the government, the Commission set up to evaluate the system felt unable to endorse the chosen method prior to the 2004 Local Government and European elections. A subsequent report gave qualified approval to the system, subject to software changes that would strengthen the integrity of the counting process.

Inevitably, against such a background the idea of nationwide e-voting in the 2007 general election was abandoned. Now it's back to square one, minus three, with the voters of Dublin North, Dublin West and Meath reverting in the twenty-first century – in Bertie Ahern's words – to 'being the laughing stock with our stupid oul' pencils'.

What must have seemed like a good and simple idea to Noel Dempsey in his days as Minister for the Environment is now in danger of being lost, certainly in its present form, in a welter of continuing argument about verification, paper trails, integrity and reliability, not to mention recrimination over the €52 million price-tag to buy the thing in the first place.

If the present Government, or a variation of it, is returned, the Minister for the Environment of the day will probably try to revive the project by moving early to secure all-party agreement on – wait for it – another Commission to decide if the system can be re-launched with any degree of confidence.

If there is a change of government, and even if there is not, the present opposition may well argue that the proposed e-voting system is tainted beyond retrieval and should be scrapped. Why would they spend some of their precious political capital reviving a system they have damned repeatedly as untrustworthy and the most blatant example of arrogance and profligacy on the part of their predecessors?

Given that the system is said to have a life-span of twenty years – almost half of which has already passed since the government bought into the idea – one suspects we will either have e-voting in the third general election of the twenty-first century or we may well wait for several elections before a government considers replacing a technology that became obsolete before it was taken out of its wrapping. In other words, if the system for which we've already paid over €50 million isn't being used, a government would be very wary of making haste on finding an alternative that would in all likelihood cost a lot more again by the time it was up and running.

Of course, it is possible to envisage circumstances in which an administration could be forced by the courts to address the issue. If, for example, a candidate defeated by a handful of votes were to seek a declaration that a result was invalid on the grounds that a critical number of votes had been spoiled by neglect on the part of those running the election, who is to say the courts should not and would not order a re-ballot?

In the 2002 election seventeen contests were decided by fewer votes than the number of spoiled votes. The total number of spoiled votes was 20,707, roughly averaging at close to five hundred votes per constituency. It has been established that almost 2,000, or 9 per cent, of these spoiled votes were invalid because they were not stamped properly by the presiding officer at the polling station before being handed to the voter.

Maybe it's the pressure of the teatime rush, but through absolutely no fault of their own up to fifty electors in each constituency are deprived of their votes as a result of human error and incompetence in the polling station. It will make for intense legal argument if a candidate who loses by ten votes seeks to have a result overturned on such grounds, especially if it can be shown that an error-prone presiding officer was present in that candidate's home territory.

The overall percentage may seem small, but 20,000 votes nationally is the equivalent of three quotas and there are grounds for believing that only a small proportion of those are spoiled intentionally. Almost 85 per cent of spoiled votes were ruled out last time because they either had no number 1 or more than one number 1 marked on the ballot paper.

Another strong argument for the electronic system is that because it sifts through all the votes of a successful candidate prior to allocating a surplus, it distributes that surplus on a more proportional and therefore a fairer basis than the present manual system, in which a sample of votes is chosen for distribution.

Whether such arguments, which some may find arcane or even far-fetched, will persuade a government to revisit the issue or persuade public opinion that paper voting should be abandoned again following its reprieve is doubtful. But if there is to be further debate about e-voting, one would hope that, for the first time, serious attention will be given to the question of whether and how the people's participation in the count can be preserved.

Obviously, this is less important than the integrity and accuracy of the system itself. If a new system is introduced, however, and the returning officers in charge of the forty-three constituencies continue to operate independently of one another, it is entirely foreseeable that Election Day will be followed by a night of chaos and information gridlock at national level.

Quite simply, electronic counting will happen so fast that it will be impossible for broadcasters and their audiences to absorb and transmit anything other than the barest facts. Individual stories, triumphs, failures and drama will be lost as the media attempts to unscramble a torrent of information at national level. Difficult as that will all be for the broadcasters, one suspects that newspapers will be left in an impossible situation.

After the piloting of e-voting five years ago, one suggestion was that in order to allow time for information to be absorbed, returning officers would begin by announcing the entire first count, then take a short break before delivering the final result. That approach would certainly make things more interesting for the limited number of people present in a given count-centre, but it would do little for the wider public's chances of taking in the whole national picture, as an identical exercise would probably be taking place in several places simultaneously.

Would it not be far better – and not terribly difficult – ahead of an electronic election to devise an 'Operation Freeflow' for the count, starting with the principal that there should be the maximum possible public access, via traditional and new media? Why shouldn't the results in Donegal North East, Cork South West and Galway East get the same national attention as those of Dublin South or Cork North Central? In tabloid terms, the Head of the Department of the Environment's franchise section would become a very visible 'Count Tsar', or 'Supremo'. His first decision might well be to regionalise the counting of votes at appointed count-centres in the same way as many Dublin constituencies are counted at the RDS. Perhaps the model of the four European constituencies would be suitable, or maybe more regional count-centres would be needed.

By using regional count-centres, linked to a national count-centre in, say, Dublin Castle, it would be easier to schedule each constituency's count and call it in at an appointed time. Anyone who wanted to, from anywhere in the world, could follow the entire proceedings on radio, television or the internet. There might be an understandable reluctance to commit to tight timetabling, but slippage time could be built into the schedule.

It should be possible to announce the outcome from a different constituency every fifteen or twenty minutes. That would make for a ten-hour marathon, which might not appeal to the candidates, who would want for nothing more than to 'get it over with' as quickly as possible after the polls closed. There's no reason why some constituencies, particularly in Dublin, couldn't be counted on election night.

One can already hear the objection: 'It's not a reality TV show we're having, or the Eurovision Song Contest, it's an *election*.'

Well, actually, if you think about it, election counts have been the greatest and most genuine 'reality TV' show since the medium was invented! What's more, Ireland's combination of multi-seat constituencies and transferable voting just happen to give us a really interesting version. There is no need to apologise if, in the interests of public access, we arrange the delivery of results in a way that provides drama, excitement, tension and – yes – entertainment. Like the 'Eurovision Song Contest', it would give us information in a way that is comprehensible, enjoyable and easy to follow. That, surely, is the best way of all to engage and educate the public. Handled properly, it is just possible that e-voting could do for election coverage what 'Riverdance' did for Irish dancing. I have almost convinced myself we should go for it!

Since 1995 Sean O'Rourke has been programme editor and presenter of 'News at One' on RTÉ Radio 1. In 2003 Sean began presenting 'The Week in Politics', a weekly review of political events on RTÉ 1. Awarded Radio Journalist of the Year in 1997, Sean will anchor the election results programme on RTÉ Radio 1 in 2007.

IV. It's Showtime

Charlie Bird

Some weeks after the November 1992 general election, in which Albert Reynolds and Fianna Fáil scraped back into power with the Labour party on the back of the so-called Spring Tide, one of the most distinguished journalists around, Gerry Barry, wrote an article in the *Sunday Tribune* revealing that Fianna Fáil had 'no tracking polls'. I was gob-smacked.

I had been assigned by RTÉ to cover the Albert Reynolds' general election tour. It was particularly interesting given that this was Albert's first time leading his party into a general election campaign as Taoiseach. (In February of that year, Charlie Haughey had been forced to stand down and Reynolds had succeeded him as leader of Fianna Fáil and as Taoiseach.) Indeed, I will never forget the first day of the campaign when we travelled to Killarney, County Kerry. The joke that night from Sean Duignan, Government Press Secretary, was that Albert was already in trouble and that I had received a better reception on the streets of Killarney than the Taoiseach.

Within days it had become apparent that the Fianna Fáil campaign was going off the rails. Every morning, along with the newspaper reporters and colour writers, I'd meet up with the Fianna Fáil campaign team and head off to wherever the Taoiseach was going. Occasionally the starting-point would be Fianna Fáil party headquarters in Dublin's Mount Street. There the Taoiseach and the handlers had early morning meetings to plan strategy as the campaign unfolded and as the opinion polls brought more and more bad news for the party.

'Diggie', as Sean Duignan was affectionately known, would come out onto the steps of Fianna Fáil HQ to shoot the breeze with the waiting journalists. On the mornings when the latest opinion polls were ominous for Fianna Fáil and for Albert, Diggie would be asked for a comment. He would explain to us, in great detail, that Fianna Fáil's own 'tracking polls' showed a very different picture. Duignan would tell us that their own polls showed the party to be in a much stronger position.

Indeed, such was the slickness of the Fianna Fáil election machine that the party brought over a media guru from Saatchi & Saatchi in London to advise on how to handle aspects of the campaign. The heavy-hitting Saatchi & Saatchi man, Steve Hilton, had also been offering advice to the Tory party in England.

When news leaked out that Fianna Fáil had a Saatchi & Saatchi man on board, and given that it was so novel at the time, great efforts were made to try and track him down. Eventually we got pictures of the mystery 'spin-doctor' while he was on the campaign trail with Albert in West Cork. Indeed, the same Steve Hilton is today one of the main full-time advisors to the new Tory leader, David Cameron.

If the opinion polls weren't bringing any good news for Fianna Fáil and for Albert Reynolds, outwardly the party was putting on a brave face. The mantra from Diggie was always the same: 'Our own opinion polls are telling us a different story. Things are going well.' Behind the façade, however, Fianna Fáil knew things weren't running smoothly. Frank Dunlop, who had been a media advisor to Jack Lynch and Charlie Haughey, was brought back on board to help shore up the defences. Such was the disarray that Albert

Reynolds telephoned him directly and asked him to drop everything and take over the running of the campaign.

It was all to no avail. In the November poll Fianna Fáil lost nine seats and dropped five percentage points. The advice from Saatchi & Saatchi, and even their favourable 'tracking polls', could not stop what was coming down the line.

Of course, in my naivety, I was shocked to read the Gerry Barry story in the *Sunday Tribune* and the news that there were no bona fide tracking polls. I had worked with Sean Duignan at RTÉ. He was a senior colleague and one of the most colourful and popular people in the business. If he told me there were tracking polls, I had no reason to doubt him. So reading the *Tribune* story, I realised how gullible I had been. In war, truth is the first casualty; the same might also be said of general elections.

Years later I was told that the so-called tracking polls were in fact reports from Fianna Fáil campaign directors around the country telling the party HQ that their door-to-door canvass reports were returning good feedback. These reports were turned into tracking polls in order to give a different, or better, spin to the news coming out from the opinion polls carried out on behalf of the national newspapers.

When Fianna Fáil launched its campaign back in 2002 another colourful character on the political scene at the time, P.J. Mara, is quoted as saying, 'It's showtime'. Once the general election campaign 2007 is up and running, that's exactly what it will be: showtime.

The late High Court judge Sean O'Leary, who was a highly respected Fine Gael handler, once told a colleague of mine who had recently been appointed Fine Gael's Director of Elections for a campaign in the 1980s: 'Don't believe anything I say for the next three weeks.' It is a good way for the media and the public to approach the forthcoming general election coverage: take everything that is said in the heat of the campaign with a good dose of salt and scepticism.

Covering the party leader's tour during a general election can be fun, but the nature of the assignment has changed dramatically over the years. Gone are the days of the church-gate meetings when the visiting party leader, flanked by the party candidates, would get up onto the back of a lorry and deliver forth on the issues of the day to those leaving church after Mass. Almost all of that razzmatazz has gone out of our politics.

Today the leaders' tours are all about ticking off the boxes. On the basis that all politics is local, it is important that the party leader is seen and photographed with all of his or her election candidates in every constituency. Another imperative is to provide the national media with their soundbite of the day and, just as importantly, to interact with the local media. Given the significance of the local media today, especially local radio, all of the party leaders' tours have exclusive time given over to an interview with the local radio station.

The 'donut' is another important part of any tour. This is where the local candidates stick as close as possible to their leader to ensure they appear in every media shot. And where would we be without the placard-carriers? It is a pre-requisite of any visit to any place that party supporters carrying posters of the leader, or the various party candidates, are placed strategically behind the leader to give the impression of a large turnout of supporters and to make sure the backdrop looks busy and bustling.

During Bertie Ahern's first leader's tour, in 1997, I noticed that Fianna Fáil had got this down to an art form. Every time Bertie went on the road, even as leader of the opposition, he would be accompanied by a number of media handlers. Maurice O'Donoghue was the tour manager. He went ahead to every location to make sure everything was arranged and nothing was out of place. Marty Whelan, from the Party Press Officer, was there to deal with 'us, the media'.

The Party General Secretary, Pat Farrell, was also on the road. Pat watched from a distance to make sure there were no glitches or gaps and that nothing was left to chance. He seemed to have the job of ensuring that any images that might make Bertie look stupid or silly, and which would appear in the evening news coverage and on the front pages of the daily papers the next morning, were not allowed to happen. Then there was Eileen Gleeson, who ran her own Public Relations company. Eileen was also on the road with Bertie Ahern and was in overall change of the media campaign.

Some images are good for a party leader, others are not. Two examples come to mind.

Late in the 1997 campaign, Bertie Ahern was on the hustings in Galway when a young female student approached him on the street and gave him a real smacker on the lips. I don't for one moment believe it was an arranged photo opportunity, but the image was captured and appeared on the front pages of the newspapers the next day. The famous 'kiss on the lips' was a talking point for days afterwards and did Bertie's street credibility no harm at all.

The same cannot be said for Michael Noonan during the 2002 general election campaign. On the front page of *The Irish Times*, on 1 May, was a photograph of a young woman throwing a custard pie into Mr Noonan's face as he arrived in Boyle, County Roscommon. In the three weeks of that election campaign, it was the only action photograph of the Fine Gael leader on the hustings.

It was not the most edifying image for Michael Noonan. During the same period Bertie Ahern had five photographs on the election trail featured in the *Irish Times*. The Fianna Fáil tour managers are always on the lookout, making sure their man never ends up on the front pages of the papers looking stupid.

The truth is that much of what is happening in our election campaigns now is being imported from the USA, where media stage-management has been honed to perfection and where nothing is left to chance.

Weclome to the world of the rebuttal unit!

During the 1997 election campaign, Fianna Fáil was the first Irish political party to set up a rebuttal unit. The idea was imported from New Labour in Britain, which in turn had copied it from Washington. The rebuttal unit comprised a number of people in election headquarters who monitored all radio and television news output. Within minutes of hearing an opposition party news story on a particular topic, Fianna Fáil would counter immediately with a statement of its own, put out in the name of one of the candidates. The effect was that every time their political opponents issued a statement or made a comment, the rebuttal unit swung into action and issued a counter-statement. So successful was the rebuttal unit that when Fianna Fáil won the 1997 election, they established a permanent one in Government Buildings.

In the 1997 campaign, and again in 2002, Fianna Fáil employed the services of a Washington DC-based company to advise on election strategy. It is believed that a number of people from Shrum Divine & Donilon, who operated in the background during both campaigns, might be in evidence this time around.

Fine Gael has also been getting some strategy advice in recent times from a Washington-based campaign expert. It will be interesting to see what new tactics the two main parties will employ in the forthcoming election. If the Fine Gael election campaign was a shambles the last time around, the same is unlikely to happen on this occasion. The party has a whole new election team, headed this time by Frank Flannery.

One thing that will be interesting to observe will be the timing of the daily party election news conferences. In the 2002 campaign, Fine Gael was the first to hold theirs each morning, followed an hour or so later by Fianna Fáil. That turned out to be a mistake for Fine Gael, giving Fianna Fáil the opportunity to rebut anything said by their opponents. Watch closely: Fine Gael are unlikely to make the same mistake again.

Finally, it is also worth remembering that during the last campaign only one opinion poll predicted the outcome correctly. Also remember the mantra of all party leaders when asked for comments on any opinion poll: there is only one poll that counts, and that's the one on Election Day.

On that we can all agree.

Charlie Bird joined RTÉ in 1974 as a researcher in Current Affairs. After six years he joined the Newsroom as a reporter, where he is now Chief News Correspondent. Since joining the RTÉ Newsroom he has covered stories within the country and around the globe. He loves his work and describes himself as a 'newsaholic'.

V. Getting voting right

Cathal MacCoille

If you had a right to vote in the last general election, you probably took it for granted. You could be sure that your vote in a fairly run process to choose your TDs was there for you to use, or to ignore. Not anymore.

Trust in the electoral register as a fair and accurate record of those entitled to vote – apart from the recently deceased – is a thing of the past. Since the 2002 general election, confusion has developed concerning five voting issues:

1. How many citizens are not on the electoral register who ought to be on it?

2. How many names are on the register that ought to have been removed?

3. How fairly elected will the next Dáil be, after preliminary census returns revealed that the TD:citizen ratio will range from 10 per cent below average to 21 per cent above it?

4. Will any of the above questions lead to the electoral system being challenged in court before, during, or after the 2007 general election?

5. How should we vote? The electronic voting system has been ruled out for 2007, but the issue is likely to arise again.

None of these clouds darkened the political landscape in 2002. Progress beckoned as the government began implementing its decision to end manual voting. Two years earlier, after the announcement had been made, the then Minister for the Environment Noel Dempsey told me on radio that paper-and-pencil elections were both slow and bad for our image as a modern, high-tech country. Yes, they made for great spectator sport, he said, but politicians were not there to provide election night drama. Broadcasters could find other ways of making elections interesting.

The shambles that followed the USA presidential election in 2000 – when Al Gore 'won', but lost – served as a warning of how machines weren't necessarily perfect. Still, choosing a new system here that would avoid the chaos of Florida's 'hanging chads' was hardly impossible. Nor was there any valid comparison, surely, between our electoral register and that of the United States, which was so poorly funded and administered that it seemed calculated more to exclude voters than to include them.

These potential problems in our electoral system were not even discussed as our e-voting machines arrived. In the 2002 general election they were used on a pilot basis in the constituencies of Meath, Dublin North and Dublin West. Everything worked smoothly, both at polling stations and at the count-centres. On my way west to present TG4's election night programme, I stopped to chat to the nation's first e-voters at a polling station in Enfield, County Meath. There were no complaints, no suspicions and certainly no nostalgia for paper and pencils. I was sure I had seen the start of a new electoral era. And with it, the passing of the slow-motion drama that had fascinated all of us who like our election counts long, revealing, unpredictable and, on occasion, publicly painful for the voters' victims.

The flaws in our electoral system, both old and new, did not take long to emerge. First, criticism of the e-voting system purchased by the government led to the establishment of a Commission to conduct a limited review. The Commission, chaired by High Court judge Matthew Smith, reported in 2004 that it could not satisfy itself as to the accuracy and reliability of the proposed system. It also reported that experts had found it 'very easy' to bypass the system's electronic security, to overwrite the software and, in theory at least, to gain complete control over an election count. The government decided against using the equipment, bought for over €50 million, in the 2004 Local Government and European elections.

After conducting a further assessment of the proposed system, the Commission on Electronic Voting reported in 2006 that the machines would be safe to use following minor modifications. However, it said the software, which controls both voting and counting, would have to be rewritten and, of course, tested again. For a second time the government ruled out the machines' use, this time for the 2007 general election.

An Taoiseach Bertie Ahern and Minister for the Environment Dick Roche have since restated their commitment to the machines' eventual use. Two major difficulties remain, however. First, building public confidence in the system and a political consensus for its introduction will be far from easy. Secondly, it appears the system that the government purchased has a weakness that cannot be rectified by any electronic system currently in use: none is capable of providing a paper record of votes cast, which would make possible a separate audit of a computer-calculated result.

Whether e-voting ever becomes a reality in Ireland, the success of its critics should be celebrated. If manual voting and counting remain, it is because the government lost an argument with its citizens, fair and square. On the other hand, if electronic voting is ever introduced, it will be based on a much better system than the one originally proposed. Tellingly, most of its weaknesses were exposed not in Dáil Éireann but thanks to the questioning and researches of ordinary citizens. Joe McCarthy, Margaret McGaley, Irish Citizens for Trustworthy E-voting, the Irish Computer Society and other well-informed sceptics scored a remarkable victory for voters over their rulers. By any standards, it was a significant moment of citizens' empowerment.

All of these developments arose out of an attempt to improve the electoral process, at least in the eyes of the proposers. Ironically, they ran into trouble just as an unresolved pre-existing problem came to light. Unknown to most of us, there were two major 'black holes' in the electoral register. The first consisted of dead or departed voters, whose unremoved names meant, according to Dick Roche's calculation, that the electoral register listed 300,000 more 'voters' than there were adults aged over eighteen in the State; some estimates put the figure much higher. But even accepting the Minister's estimate, the implications were serious. To what use were those polling cards put? And imagine that the names of those 300,000 people who were either dead or disqualified for other reasons had been removed from the register before the 2002 general election. The turnout on Election Day would then have been not 62 per cent – the lowest since 1923 – but a respectable 68 per cent.

The second 'black hole', and the need to find out how many potential voters it contained, should have been obvious as the rate of new house- and apartment-building in the State approached 90,000 units a year. Despite the unprecedented pace of building, until recently there had been no concerted effort to ensure that new voters were detected and added to the electoral register.

The scale of both problems was first uncovered by Shane Coleman and Odran Flynn, of the *Sunday Tribune*, in June 2005.

Further evidence of the consequences of neglect was provided by Fianna Fáil's Trinity College *cumann* last year. A survey carried out by its members in Dublin South-East estimated that some 17,000 people who were entitled to vote were not on the electoral register. Almost as seriously, their research concluded that, in just one constituency alone, 15,000 people who had either died or moved house were still registered as voters.

What emerged from these unofficial inquiries was a flawed register that must inevitably lower the standard of our electoral process. It is a reasonably true and accurate record of the voters' choices, but it is also a lottery that can be both unfair and unpredictable in its distorting effects. This contrasts oddly with the care and attention devoted to counting votes.

Such a failure would merit censure from Irish observers of elections in emerging democracies abroad. It certainly leaves us in no position to smugly decry the shortcomings of the American system, despite the Florida farce in 2000. As in the United States, we have had no national standard of maintaining or updating our electoral register. As in the United States, freak results are likely, albeit less likely, to be detected. Perhaps more likely, indeed, given the fact that under proportional representation winning margins can be as small as Dan Neville's of Fine Gael in Limerick West – one vote – or John Dennehy's of Fianna Fáil in Cork South Central – six votes – in the last general election.

Even assuming that most voting cards issued to non-voters are not misused, they present an obvious danger, both locally and nationally. Given that a few thousand votes often decide the formation of governments, it is not hard to see the potential for mischief of even a few thousand improper votes.

Despite its flaws, the recent campaign to update the register has brought about a degree of welcome improvement. Last year, the names of 380,000 voters not previously registered at their address were added to the electoral roll. There have been more than half-a-million corrections and deletions. These related to the names of people who had died, moved residence, were on the register more than once, or with whom, as Dick Roche delicately put it in the Dáil on 28 November 2006, 'the councils were unable to establish contact'. This figure included Labour TD Jack Wall, who, bizarrely, was removed from the register in Kildare South while his wife and daughter, who live at the same address, kept their votes. On Election Day 2007, who knows how many genuine voters will make a similarly unwelcome discovery at their local polling station.

The checking process has also highlighted how local authorities are managing the register differently. To take two neighbouring examples: nearly one-quarter of the names on the Meath register were removed as a result of last year's check-up, but only one-seventh of the names on the register in Louth. Such a substantial difference can only mean either that the Meath register was far more inaccurate beforehand or that the Louth check-up was not as rigorous. Either way, the inconsistency shows the need for a national standard of voter registration and checking. That is unlikely to emerge as long as the job is left to local authorities.

The General Election 2007 will give us a measure of the quality of the work done on the electoral register in the last year-and-a-half. It is already clear that the electorate, as listed on the electoral register, is still much larger (at least 100,000 larger, and probably more) than the population of qualified adults. No matter how the excess is calculated, the implied defects are serious. Why?

Because the number of names on any voluntary electoral register, if properly updated, should be less than the number of qualified voters. If it is higher, there can be only one cause: the job isn't being done right.

In fairness to Dick Roche, it should be remembered that he has been Minister for the Environment and Local Government only since September 2004. His was the first nationally organised attempt to clean up the register after decades of neglect. As a result, this election will undoubtedly provide us with a fairer and more accurate measure of the electorate's opinion than that held on 17 May 2002.

The limited extent of the improvement, however, was revealed to me by conversations with two Dublin voters last autumn. Their names had been deleted from the register, even though neither was deceased, had left the country, had changed address, had received any form or correspondence from their local authority, had been visited by anyone representing their local authority or been informed subsequently that their names had been deleted. Their experiences, like that of Jack Wall, suggest that more resources should have been applied to the exercise.

This seems even more obvious if the numbers employed to carry out the 2006 census are compared with the numbers engaged in checking the electoral register: 4,840 for the census; just 1,500 to update the electoral register. It seems clear that more resources and a better checking system are needed if the mess is ever to be sorted out. For example, the use of personal public service (PPS) numbers, as in Northern Ireland, which was ruled out during the recent exercise here, seems worth looking at again.

The task may soon be dealt with by a national electoral commission, a growing consensus for which has emerged from among the parties as the recent débacle unfolded. The controversies over e-voting and voter registration may have created a fair wind for such a body.

None of this reduces the obligation on voters to put their names on the electoral register and to check that they have not been deleted. If your name is missing, remember, you have a Minister's guarantee that you can still get a vote, even after the official election campaign begins. As Dick Roche said in the Dáil on 28 November 2006:

> 'People may get on the supplement to the register up to fifteen days before polling day. Nobody is being disenfranchised and every voter who wishes to get on the register between now and the fifteenth day before the general election may do so with relative ease.'

Electronic voting is an issue that will return in the future. Like most broadcasters, I find the prospect depressing. Because it will telescope election-count coverage into a few hours, in which results will emerge too quickly to be analysed properly. Because the national result will receive more attention than the local results that led to it, because discussion of what it all means will be cut short by the speed of the process. And, of course, because it threatens the drama and excitement that most of us – politicians excepted – enjoy. All over in an hour or two may suit politicians, but who said elections were for their convenience?

There is a separate objection to the end of manual voting. At a manual count, the voters' verdict is literally observable. If you were an activist in, say, Carlow–Kilkenny, you can see how your candidate is doing in Thomastown, or have a look at the tally. If the other crowd is getting transfers in Fiddown, they, and you, can see the transfer pattern, and everyone else can be kept informed.

The count-centre is also the forum where opposing candidates and their supporters gather – mainly, of course, to find out what the voters have decided, but also to experience something that is almost as important. They want be part of the (usually) friendly, or at least civilised, atmosphere, the congratulating of victors and sympathy for losers, the shared tally, the polite listening to speeches, the joy and disappointment – all that and more are key elements of democracy. Respect for opponents and for voters is part of the process. Rush the count, as people head off to celebrate with their own, and we may degrade some of the warp and the weft of our politics.

To end, a second, but I promise brief, bout of special pleading. My job is to ask questions. Listeners don't forget politicians who dodge questions, or who steer clear of programmes like 'Morning Ireland' rather than answer hard questions. There is, however, one question I would like to be able to ask about voters. Transparency and accountability should work both ways. Electing, like being elected, is public business. Shouldn't there be a right in Ireland to access information about voters such as is available, for example, in the United States?

I am not proposing a right to know *how* people voted, but a right to know *whether* they voted. Here, such information is collected unofficially and often on a haphazard basis by some parties in some constituencies. There is also an official record, but that is available solely for the purpose of election challenges and is destroyed after six months. In the USA, a journalist can check, for example, whether a voter who is complaining about a politician cast his/her vote in the last election. If the same system applied here, I could not check the accuracy of your claim to have voted for a TD whose subsequent actions you say have disappointed you, but I could check whether you voted. Why do I want to know? Because several TDs have told me they know of people who assured them they had voted for them, even though the TDs knew they never entered their local polling station on Election Day. As a journalist, I'd like access to that information, too.

Most American states restrict access to voting records to those whose curiosity is deemed to be in the public interest, such as political parties, public campaign groups and the media. In Florida, for example, a CD-Rom containing a record of all voters' participation in all elections since 2000 is available for $9.99. Why not allow access to the same information here?

Cathal MacCoille is one of the three presenters of RTÉ's flagship Radio News programme, 'Morning Ireland'. He is a former Political Correspondent for TG4. He currently writes a political column for the Irish-language weekly, *Foinse*. In 1990 he won a Jacob's Radio Award. He will chair TG4's election results programme in 2007.

VI. Not so PC

Pat Kenny

My heart goes out to the politicians, the men and women of the current Dáil. They climbed aboard the rollercoaster almost five years ago and their trolley, which has chugged along steadily up to this, is now just centimetres away from the very top of the Big Dipper. As they go screaming down the tracks, will they have enough momentum to take them back up the other side, safe in their seats, or will their baggage weigh them down and throw them off the rails, spinning to political oblivion?

To borrow a useful phrase from the Lotto – 'It Could Be You!' Facing an election is like being pregnant: you know there is potentially a wonderful outcome, with congratulations all round, but first you've got to go through the painful business of childbirth. And there is no other way. Be you Taoiseach, Tánaiste or humble back-bencher, the path to glory is just the same: you must prostrate yourself at the feet of your electorate. Of the 166 TDs, 165 of them face weeks of uncertainty – although, in truth, a handful will be 1,000 per cent safe. Only the 166th, the Ceann Comhairle, is returned unopposed, so that's definitely the best job in the place. And although Bertie has been good to them, with job security for five whole years, benchmarked salaries, great pensions and soft financial landings for those who won't make it in 2007, they must really hate the impending general election.

On the other hand, we, the voters, all love general elections. The body politic is energised. The opposition parties, which couldn't get a look-in for five years, now see their policies and their personalities being examined seriously because *they* just might be running the show in a few weeks' time. At the moment there is an avalanche of policies and promises. The stakes are high. The Celtic Tiger appears a bit skittish these days. Who do you elect to steady the ship?

The sheer unpredictability of the whole thing makes it a lot like sport. On a good day, the underdog can just about pull off an upset. As the results unfold there will be tears, cheers and jeers as household names are upended by the voters, and outsiders come cantering home. It has always been so – every single general election has produced shocks as seemingly safe seats become alarmingly unsafe. Over the years we have watched Nora Owen, Dick Spring, Niamh Breathnach, the late Brian Lenihan, his sister Mary O'Rourke, Michael McDowell and many more fall by the wayside against the run of play. The well-padded leather upholstery of a 'state car' offers no insurance against the triple-whammy of your party going out of government, your ministerial portfolio going to your tormentor from the opposite side of the house and your basic job, your seat, going to some upstart, sometimes even a member of your own party. Oh, the ignominy of it all.

Of course, that is why we, the voters, watch the results unfold on television in huge numbers. By contrast, the elections in Britain are almost perfunctory affairs. There is likely to be more drama in one episode of 'EastEnders' than in an entire election campaign over there. The first-past-the-post system in Britain means that the pre-election polls really do predict the winner, and the only real entertainment is in watching the likes of a Michael Portillo get a mugging from his constituents. Naturally there is drama in a change of government, but even then the choreography is pre-ordained and low-key: driven to the count in a ministerial Jag, lose the fight and within hours you have lost your home, and you retreat to your constituency in a party Mondeo. It's a ruthless and pitiless business.

In Ireland, on the other hand, it's not so much the story as the way it's told. It explains why we love the PR system, and why e-voting turned us off. A computer telling us in seconds, rather than hours or days, how a count is going leaves us feeling cheated. There is no nuance, no false dawns, no hopes raised only to be dashed – the computer sucks the very life out of the thing. Of course, there are computers and there are computers, as there are horses for courses. We in RTÉ use computers for a number of jobs. We use them to generate nice images, startling graphical representations of, for example, the State of the Parties, the swings this way and that, the filling up of a virtual Dáil Chamber in the PJ Maravid colours never actually seen in the House, except in the royal blue of the carpet. We also use computers to predict the result as increasing numbers of constituencies declare, and we use computers to generate all the numbers about second , third and fourth preferences and the destinations of surpluses or eliminations, so that the eminent panels can have all the relevant facts to inform and entertain us. So we are utterly dependent on the humble microchip to be able to do the job at all. And, to be fair, we have rarely been let down. But it has happened, and when it goes wrong, it goes gloriously wrong!

I bring you back to 1987. The coalition government of Garret FitzGerald's Fine Gael and Dick Spring's Labour had collapsed. In RTÉ it was all hands to the pump. But in the frenzy of preparation for the huge setpiece of television that is general election coverage, there was one light on the technical horizon that was going to make our job a lot easier: the computer. The new computer software was going to integrate the whole thing. Before that, we had a software package that would produce the graphics, but the information had to be fed into it, count by count. A reporter at a count-centre would telephone in the result and an operator would then feed it into the graphics package. Meanwhile the experts on the panel, with pen and paper, would figure out the whole thing. Remember, this was in a time before a PC adorned every desk and before the mobile phone had arrived.

In fact, it wasn't long since we had prepared all the graphics on cardboard cards and literally placed them on what were called caption stands in front of the camera. But now we were going to be able to simply feed the count results into the computer, it would crunch the numbers and push them out the other end in different formats for the different end-users. One set of numbers would go directly into the graphic generator, another set would be spewed out on paper for the pundits to parse, a third set would go to the Newsdesk and so on. So this computer stuff was the business!

Nowadays, of course, we are all computer literate, and equally we know not to trust them blindly. We frequently have to reboot for no apparent reason and we make back-ups of all our data. If we are worldly wise in the ways of technology now, back then we were the foolish virgins.

I was asked to be one of the anchors for RTÉ's televison coverage. While Brian Farrell grilled his guests, I simply had to bring the latest information on the various counts to the viewers as the information came to hand on the graphics display. To help me with this I had 'the most sophisticated computer software package ever seen on Irish television!!' Little did we know, it was going to be a long night.

In addition to a preview screen where I might be shown results just before we presented them to the public, I had an earpiece in my right ear through which the director would communicate with me. In the middle of a result sequence I might be told to go straight to Cork for a live declaration, or whatever. We were determined to be on the ball. To prepare for my task, I decided to ask for one extra facility. The little extra I asked for that night was another earpiece, this one containing a live feed of RTÉ Radio 1's results coverage.

The early hours of results coverage are tedious. I had little enough to do. A long piece at the beginning of the programme laying out our technical stall, explaining the way our graphics would tell the unfolding story, cueing in a few tallies, waiting until the first hard information began to come in. Then, as afternoon turned to evening, the trickle of results became a flood and I was really busy.

The counts came thick and fast. Unlike in Britain, where you have only one declaration for a constituency, in Ireland there is count after count – a result of a surplus distribution and elimination and distribution of preferences until, ultimately, somebody is elected ... and that's only the beginning. Because of our multi-seat constituencies there are many, many counts, so that a returning officer will become as familiar as an old friend before the night is out.

I don't know when exactly it all started to go pear-shaped. All I do know is that results began popping up on the screen that seemed a bit odd to me. I passed the word back to the control room that I thought something was amiss, but nobody thought that was possible. After all, there was no possibility of human error.

The stuff was coming directly from THE COMPUTER, for God's sake!

I continued reading the stuff, as given, for a few more minutes, but my suspicions were soon confirmed. I had been giving results of counts from Dublin West, the constituency of the late Brian Lenihan. Brian had been elected about an hour previously. But lo and behold, there on the screen, a result for Dublin West and no sign of the bould Brian at all! Live on air I told the viewers not to believe a word of it, that Brian Lenihan had already been elected and that there was certainly at least one less seat to fill than our own screen indicated. More followed. The computer boffins continued to put results up on screen, I would start to read them only to pause and say, 'This cannot be correct. I think the computer has got this one wrong.' It was high-wire stuff! But my certainty that something was radically wrong was being confirmed by a source only I was plugged into: all the time, in my left ear, I had the output of RTÉ Radio 1.

The battle between me and the computer continued on air for quite a while – a couple of hours, I imagine – until finally the producer had to accept that the software was fatally flawed. We abandoned the microchip. It was back to cardboard caption cards for the rest of the night!

Our mini-crisis was as nothing compared to a change of government and the return of Charles J Haughey, but I remember it far more vividly than the politics of the evening. In subsequent elections most of the presenters were equipped with that radio feed, and in truth there is a sort of friendly battle between the Radio and Television Divisions to be first with a count result, or even with a prediction of the outcome. The only problem is that nowadays we are all plugged into the same results computer. The numbers are fed from that computer to radio, to television, to Aertel and to www.rte.ie. Yes, we all are fed from the same source. Now, just suppose that sat down? But it couldn't, of course. After all, it's a computer, isn't it?

Pat Kenny is one of Ireland's foremost broadcasters. Over a number of elections he was part of the RTÉ television team on results night. He is the presenter of 'Today with Pat Kenny', a daily talk and current affairs show on RTÉ Radio 1. He also hosts 'The Late, Late Show', one of the country's most popular television programmes.

VII. The Albert Factor

Fergal Keane

Mid-November 1992 and things were not going well for Fianna Fáil. Ten days into a snap election campaign, the party was floundering in the polls and, under the leadership of Albert Reynolds, was facing into serious seat losses.

It was a Friday and it had been a tough week for the Taoiseach; a mad dash through nearly twenty constituencies had been a demoralising experience. The crowds were not turning out and Albert himself often seemed ill-at-ease on the canvass. There was talk that 'the Albert Factor' was in play, that people believed they were being asked to vote in an unnecessary election and that Albert Reynolds was to blame.

This particular Friday, in Kells, in 'The Royal County of Meath', the word had gone out from party headquarters that greater efforts had to be made. Fianna Fáil in County Meath was not going to be found wanting. Arriving into town, the Taoiseach was greeted by all the party candidates in the constituency. A large, red, open-top Mercedes was produced and he was pressed to sit in the back, JFK-style, flanked by the two women candidates, Mary Wallace and Frances Monaghan.

As the car moved off slowly through the empty streets of Kells the two local FF TDs, Noel Dempsey and Colm Hilliard, jogged alongside it, for all the world like a Secret Service deployment. To add a bit of showbiz, they were followed closely by a large white van with speakers on top, blaring out Irish music at such a volume you could barely hear yourself think.

As this strange parade moved through the town, Albert Reynolds was looking decidedly embarrassed. Up ahead, party workers were knocking on doors and dragging reluctant voters from their warm homes to meet the Taoiseach. Elderly women were helped across the street for a chat with the leader of the country and one bemused gent, walking his fat Labrador and minding his own business, was prevailed upon to stop and discuss the affairs of state.

It all proved too much for the Labrador. Driven demented by the loud 'jigs 'n' reels' and by the excitement of meeting the Taoiseach, he barked his head off, chased his tail and tried to climb into the car – no doubt wanting to make the personal acquaintance of the founder of the C&D pet-food empire.

Later, as Mr Reynolds posed for photographers in a nearby supermarket, having his picture taken with a basket of shopping, sliced pans, chicken legs and bananas, the Government Press Secretary asked the few journalists lucky enough to have witnessed one of the great scenes of Irish electioneering what we thought. He himself said he felt it was all a bit over the top, but I assured him it had been one of the greatest things I had ever seen in my life. In retrospect, if I had had my wits about me, I would have invented 'Father Ted' on the spot.

That is how it was for Albert Reynolds in 1992. This was an Albert Reynolds prior to the IRA ceasefire and the Downing Street Declaration, prior to his playing a central role in brokering a deal in Northern Ireland. In those few November weeks he was fighting for his political life. The coalition government with the Progressive Democrats, which he had inherited from Charles Haughey, had collapsed acrimoniously following an ongoing row between the Taoiseach and the Tánaiste, Des O'Malley, over evidence each man had given to the Beef Tribunal. People were blaming Albert.

Polls showed that people didn't believe his version of events. An Irish Marketing Surveys poll just a couple of days into the general election campaign showed that 56 per cent of voters did not accept the evidence he had given at the Tribunal, while another 22 per cent said they didn't know. The Fianna Fáil vote was dropping below 40 per cent, he looked like becoming the shortest-serving leader of the party in its history and the strain was beginning to show.

It had all begun so differently the previous February. When Seán Doherty made his allegations about Charles Haughey's state of knowledge in the telephone-tapping scandal ten years earlier, Haughey was gone in weeks. The 'Longford Leader' took over, promising open and transparent government and a clean new start. He immediately instigated the most savage cull of senior ministers anyone could remember. In an unforgettable fifteen minutes he fired Ray Burke, Gerry Collins, Mary O'Rourke, Rory O'Hanlon, Brendan Daly, Vincent Brady, Michael O'Kennedy and Noel Davern. Nine out of twelve junior ministers followed them out the door. 'You just backed the wrong horse,' Reynolds told them, who himself had been sacked by Haughey just a few months before. In the election that was to follow, just seven months down the road, several of them neither forgive nor forgot.

Open government was something everyone believed would come naturally to Albert Reynolds. He was always friendly and approachable, so unlike Haughey; and he always gave off an air of certainty, that he made decisions and stuck to them and seemed comfortable with that. While he was Minister for Finance, and later when he challenged Charles Haughey for the leadership, journalists often phoned his home to throw a few questions at him. Even on the eve of a Budget he might take your call. At the very least his family would be polite and friendly to you.

As part of the open government policy, and no doubt motivated in part by his relaxed attitude towards the media, he agreed early on to have an hour-long question-and-answer session with political correspondents in their office in Leinster House once a week. The 'pol corrs' room is a cramped double office hidden away in one of the top corners of Leinster House, into which the cream of the country's political journalists are shoe-horned, to work almost on top of one other. The working conditions there are so poor that many inhabitants believe it is the politicians' way of getting back at them for all they have written and reported over the years. Even now, no politician would dare step into that den and lay him or herself open to questions, but it was obvious that Albert Reynolds felt he had nothing to hide and nothing would go wrong.

In his book on his time as Government Press Secretary in the Reynolds' administration, Sean Duignan said that all journalists eventually bite the hand that feeds them. It's nothing personal, it's just the way they are. They get a bit bored and bite, maybe just to see what happens, a bit like rabid dogs.

So it was for Albert Reynolds. The first few months of his administration appeared to lurch from one crisis to the next. Less than two weeks in office and the 'X' case exploded all over the front pages. A fourteen-year-old rape victim was barred by the High Court from travelling to the United Kingdom to secure an abortion after the Government law officer, Attorney-General Harry Whelehan, took a case against her. The newspapers on one side and the Church on the other laid into the Taoiseach, and the fallout from the case rumbled on for months. His relationship with the media wasn't helped by the libel writs issued on his behalf if a journalist got something wrong. At various times he was in dispute with *The Irish Times*, RTÉ, the *Sunday Times* and others.

In the space of a few months many reporters came to the view that he was not really in control, a view helped along the way by some of his utterances. 'That's women for you now', 'Crap, total crap' and describing himself as 'a one-page man' were all hostages to fortune where the electorate was concerned.

So early into his administration, the Taoiseach could have had little idea how near the end was. The Beef Tribunal had been rumbling on for months when Tánaiste Des O'Malley took the stand. He accused Reynolds of being 'wrong, unwise, reckless and foolish' in the way he had extended export credit insurance to the Larry Goodman organisation while he was Minister for Industry and Commerce.

Reynolds was incensed, and in reality it was the end of the coalition government – something the Taoiseach had once famously described, at a party meeting in Kantar, County Cork, as a 'temporary little arrangement'. Advisors later told how he constantly flew off the handle when faced with O'Malley's evidence; the surprising thing is that the government lasted for another four months. In reality, of course, the Taoiseach was plotting his revenge.

By the time he took the stand at the Tribunal in Dublin Castle, Albert Reynolds was an embattled figure. A number of those he had culled from the front-bench hadn't backed him up in their evidence, and the relationship with the Progressive Democrats was hostile in the extreme. Accused of favouring a Fianna Fáil supporter, Goodman, at the taxpayers' expense, Reynolds hit out.

O'Malley's evidence, he said, was 'reckless, irresponsible and dishonest'.

The 'd' word took everyone by surprise, except perhaps O'Malley. Within a week of Reynolds completing days of angry and argumentative evidence, O'Malley led his party out of government and Albert Reynolds went to the country for a November election.

At the time, I was a journalist with the *Sunday Tribune* and I was assigned to follow the Taoiseach for the duration of the campaign. It's the kind of assignment journalists love: being swept around the country in cavalcades by compliant public relations people, breaking every speed limit and giving the candidates grief. On the media bus you can pass the time with savage slagging of everyone and anyone, and generally talk shop and swap gossip.

From a media perspective, the Fianna Fáil general election campaign of 2002 was the most controlled we had ever seen. Many political journalists still believe that at the time they were fooled into accepting what ministers told them and failed to see the cracks.

Back in 1992 the cracks were about all you could see. From the off, the government campaign was in disarray. It was as if Fianna Fáil, along with everyone else, had been caught by surprise by the election and was just playing it by ear. When the party grandee, PJ Mara, launched the party manifesto in 2002 in the glitzy surroundings of the Shelbourne Hotel, he did so with the words, 'It's showtime, folks.' What followed for the next three weeks was indeed a performance, but there was none of that in 1992.

The launch of the party manifesto was drowned out by news of disastrous polls. A MRBI poll in *The Irish Times* the next day, when the party plans should have been on the front pages, showed Fianna Fáil at an historic low of 40 per cent. It was a drop of 9 per cent in six weeks, while the Taoiseach had an approval rating of just 29 per cent. The *Irish Independent*'s read on the party manifesto and the spending involved was: 'Reynolds bids £750 million to buy the vote.'

When he hit the campaign trail, the omens were not good. A series of verbal gaffes in RTÉ interviews showed a man under considerable pressure, and the party seemed to be deserting him in droves. There was an air of complete panic surrounding the campaign and at times it descended into farce.

On 17 November 1992, after what was probably the worst few days of his career, the Taoiseach started his day meeting delegations of farmers in Government Buildings. He habitually greeted people like this with a step in and a handshake somewhere below waist-level and 'How are ye, lads?' – perfect for a GAA match. As one delegation left, they met up with another and exchanged jokes.

'The whole thing is collapsing like a pack of cards. Just ask and it will be granted,' one IFA delegation told the next farming group.

The message from Albert Reynolds and Fianna Fáil at the time was, 'the only way was up'.

'It's halfway over now, we're playing against the wind, but all good teams perform well against the wind,' he told those of us looking on. It was a sporting mantra he would repeat for anyone who cared to listen, right up to Election Day, but it was followed by a photo opportunity that could have ended his political aspirations in one flash, and through no fault of his own. On a visit to Our Ladies' Hospital for Sick Children in Dublin, he was accompanied by his entourage and about twenty or thirty photographers and journalists. On arrival he was met by the Minister for Health, Dr

John O'Connell, and hospital staff and told that he would be visiting the intensive care unit.

We all squashed our way into the ward and the Taoiseach was told that one of the tiny children there had just undergone heart surgery. As he is being told of the wonders of modern medicine a consultant is in the background, asking us to leave. 'There is a child here who is dying, this is a bit inappropriate,' he tells us.

Sean Duignan pleaded with the photographers to abandon the whole hospital visit as the scrum moved off into other wards and patients complained.

The next day it's Sligo and another visit to a hospital, but this time to TD Mary Coughlan, who has just had here appendix removed. A couple of hours later it's Donegal and a visit to Carndonagh Community School, the largest in the country, on the Inishowen peninsula.

Over the years there is something you begin to notice about successive taoisigh. Many of them start out awkwardly enough, as if they don't really believe that the hoopla surrounding the Office is for them, but they then grow comfortable with it and develop a star quality. Charles Haughey had that quality, a kind of aura of leadership, even though he never won an overall majority. Bertie Ahern has grown into it and is comfortable on the canvass, meeting people and seeming to engage in small-talk, even if more often that not it's nothing more than, 'Howaya, lads'.

During that general election campaign, Albert Reynolds didn't have that aura. He obviously felt uncomfortable meeting groups of people he didn't know. The schoolchildren in Carndonagh didn't know whether to cheer or blush when their principal, Brian Mullins, the former All-Ireland winning Dublin footballer, introduced Reynolds to a class. Later, when visiting the Fruit of the

Loom factory, his awkwardness was visible again: when he walks into a large crowd, he still doesn't know how to work the room and is greeted by embarrassment and a few scattered cheers.

He is at his best with a script or during media interviews, something he had years to get used to in the relative anonymity of various ministries. But being Taoiseach? This demands a lot more.

As the campaign goes on there are disappointing crowds in Carlow–Kilkenny, Clonmel, Tralee and Drogheda, just about everywhere. The campaign at times looked to be in utter chaos and his schedule could change on an hourly basis. I remember waiting on one industrial estate in Kilkenny, with workers from a new Telecom plant. The Taoiseach was due to arrive and lay a few bricks for the foundations. The site had been swept and cleaned – it was the cleanest building site in the county – and everyone was wearing new white helmets, waiting for Albert. A neat pile of bricks had been placed alongside a delicately fashioned lump of cement and a new trowel.

An hour after he was due to arrive we saw a helicopter taking off from the town. He was gone, and everyone just went off home disappointed, leaving the cement to harden in the freezing November wind.

Afterwards, party officials described how there was panic in the campaign. Frenzied phone calls were continually being made to towns ahead of the Taoiseach's cavalcade to get crowds out and not have him canvassing empty streets. There was an expectancy of disaster on Election Day and some said the Taoiseach was something of an electoral liability – unpopular with voters and likely to put his foot in it. As senior figures attempted to save themselves, what became known as the 'Albert factor' was being raised on doorsteps all over the country. The newspapers portrayed him as someone out of his depth, stumbling from one *faux pas* to another. The 'stumblebum' Taoiseach, as one put it.

Those close to him told him that he was being let down by the party machine, and that people on the ground were not turning out for him. Even though he insisted he had nothing whatsoever to do with the toppling of Haughey, it seemed the party was blaming him. According to some, he who had wielded the knife would not wear the crown for long.

On a personal level the campaign was gruelling for Albert Reynolds. He was worried about the effect the lashing he was getting in the media and on the doorsteps was having on his wife, Kathleen, who had suffered breast cancer the previous year. In an interview with the *Irish Press* she spoke of her anguish over the viciousness of the campaign:

> 'I just can't take it. I can't believe what's happened over the past few days. I can't recognise the man I married in what's being said about him. In three weeks he's gone from being the best man around to someone none of us recognise.'

But watching him as he made the rounds of the country, at times up to five constituencies a day, Reynolds seemed to be growing in his ability to work a room. Some politicians will tell you how they find canvassing and meeting people actually energises them, and the really good ones seem to draw encouragement, as well as confidence, from the public.

So it seemed for Albert Reynolds. As the three-week campaign drew to a close, he seemed to have stared into the abyss and come out the other side. By Election Day he was a measurably better politician than the one who had lost the vote of No Confidence in the Dáil, which had precipitated the election. But, of course, he also had something up his sleeve.

Reynolds told no one that he had an eye on Labour from the outset of the campaign, no one in his party and least of all Fine Gael leader John Bruton and Labour party leader Dick Spring. In the concluding debates in the Dáil he lambasted Fine Gael, but refused to respond in kind to attacks from the Labour leader. The business-dealmaker in him must have known all along that even facing meltdown at the ballot box, something could still be pulled out of the bag.

The actual result was a disaster for Fianna Fáil and exactly in line with the poll predictions. Losing nine seats and down to sixty-seven, Reynolds looked set for the back-benches. But in marked contrast to the way he would walk away two years later, he steadfastly refused to resign. A couple of days in his constituency in Longford convinced him to hang on and see what would happen.

What happened, of course, was the John Bruton overplayed his hand. His party had lost ten seats, too, but he was unwilling to give Labour what they wanted. In the face of stiff opposition from senior members of his own party who wanted to go into 'principled opposition', Reynolds outmanoeuvred Fine Gael and did a deal with Dick Spring. On 12 January, just over two months after his government collapsed, Albert Reynolds was back in Government Buildings in partnership with Labour – and with the biggest majority the Dáil had ever seen.

The following 15 December saw the signing of the Downing Street Declaration, and within months the IRA and the UVF were on ceasefire. Reynolds had brokered a deal no one really thought possible. He had cut corners, gambled, risked his and his government's reputation and played hardball with just about everyone at various times. In the end, he had played the central role in getting underway the peace process that has brought about a profound change in all our lives.

By the first anniversary of the signing of the Declaration, however, Albert Reynolds was out and John Bruton was installed as Taoiseach. If his business acumen had allowed him to cut a deal on Northern Ireland, his stubbornness had led to the collapse of a second administration after Labour pulled the plug. The 'partnership' government was built on trust, Dick Spring had always said, and that trust broke down over the leaking of the Beef Tribunal report and the Brendan Smyth affair.

Nonetheless, the intervening two years had seen possibly one of the greatest comebacks in Irish political history. From being just days away from facing a revolt by his own back-benchers, Reynolds refused to give up and was able to retire on his laurels to the international lecture circuit. In a mere twenty-four months he had gone from being the 'Longford Slasher' and the 'stumblebum Taoiseach' to being a statesman.

Fergal Keane is a reporter with RTÉ Radio 1 and was named PPAI Broadcaster of the Year in 2004. He previously worked with the *Sunday Tribune* and the *Irish Press*. He will be reporting on the 2007 election campaign for 'Drivetime' each evening on RTÉ Radio 1.

VIII. Beware of the Pundits

Derek Davis

Growing up in Bangor, County Down, elections had little
excitement and no surprises. North Down was resolutely unionist.
In those days there were no permutations of unionists – just the
Unionist party. Officially it was the Tory and Unionist party, but
the British Labour party did not organise in Northern Ireland.
There was a Northern Ireland Labour party, but it was without the
resources or obvious support of its comrades across the water.
There were some nationalist parties and an odd republican
candidate would stand as a principled no-hoper, but election
results were pre-determined by the size of the unionist majority
and a quite unnecessary gerrymander in areas with a nationalist
majority.

At election time unionist politicians with a large working-class
constituency would distract them from the government's failures
in housing and employment by conjuring up the spectre of the IRA
bogeyman. There had been a poorly supported and hugely
unsuccessful IRA campaign in the 1950s, but it was enough to give
unionist politicians a firm re-election guarantee for nearly two
decades.

In short, Northern Ireland's first-past-the-post elections were
boring and predictable. That the democratic process, as
administered by the Unionist party, would allow no political
change undoubtedly led to the Civil Rights movement of the late
1960s. In Northern Ireland the right to vote in local government
elections depended on the ownership of property or the tenancy of

public housing. When you gave a Catholic or nationalist family a house, you gave them a vote. Austin Currie of the SDLP, and later a Housing Minister himself, was one of the first to agitate against that injustice. And then there was the gerrymandering I mentioned.

The irony was that none of those abuses was necessary. There was a 60 per cent unionist majority. They didn't need any skullduggery, not with the simple first-past-the-post voting system. My MP, the one who sat in the Stormont Parliament, was Dr Nixon, a local GP. Like most of Bangor, he was an easy-going, middle-class unionist who was re-elected as a matter of course, with little or no real opposition. Dr Nixon was a nice man with a big family of free-range children, one of whom was a pal of mine. My parents were friendly with him and his wife. He was held in high regard and I believe he was quite bewildered when a group of students, myself included, lobbied him on the steps of Stormont about the abuses perpetrated by the Unionist government. Like so many moderate, decent unionists, he faded from politics in the early 1970s. Politicians were getting tougher and politics was becoming more interesting. This period saw the rise of the SDLP, the escalation of atrocious violence and my emigration south of the border.

To be honest, as an *Irish Times* reader and as a journalist I had some knowledge of politics south of the border, but no feeling for it. I had followed the arms-smuggling drama and the response of Jack Lynch's government to events in the North, but didn't feel any way involved when Liam Cosgrave took over to lead a Fine Gael/Labour coalition in 1973. By 1974 I was a reporter on the RTÉ newsdesk, with three years to go before having to grapple with the intricacies of proportional representation and multi-seat constituencies. The then Minister for the Environment was the Labour party's Jimmy Tully, an affable little man and a very astute politician. He had redrawn the constituencies during his tenure, perhaps for good democratic reasons, but it was calculated that if the coalition maintained their percentage advantage over Fianna Fáil, they would have a massive electoral victory in 1977.

Most ordinary reporters were in awe of the political correspondents and columnists. These elite journalists were in daily contact with the most powerful people in the State. They shared insiders' knowledge and wouldn't hesitate to pronounce to lesser members of the fourth estate. They thought great thoughts and talked mostly to each other. They even tended to travel together at election time. Coming up to Election Day in 1977, as I remember it, they all agreed it would be a coalition landslide.

On the day of the count I was sent to cover Dublin North County. It was a three-seater. The expert prognosis was that John Boland, a Fine Gael minister, could haul a second Fine Gael deputy over the line, leaving Ray Burke as the solitary Fianna Fáil representative. John Boland ran what was accepted by all sides as one of the best teams of tallymen in the country, and by mid-morning they were worried. What hadn't been considered were the consequences of Jimmy Tully's constituency adjustments if the swing was against Fine Gael and Labour. By noon in North County Dublin, John Boland was pale and sweating. He was also candid. 'It's going to be two Fianna Fáil and one Fine Gael,' he told me. 'And if that's the national trend, we're fecked.'

I phoned the RTÉ newsdesk and filed the copy. I also made a briefing call to one of our political experts. He was in foul form. Early tallies from other parts of the country were confirming what that three-seat barometer in North County Dublin was saying. No one likes to be wrong – not *that* wrong!

For a lot of politicians and political correspondents, it was all unravelling. Fianna Fáil was heading for its biggest ever election victory. By the time darkness fell, even with lots of results to be ratified and declared, it was accepted by all that Fianna Fáil would form the next government. Experts were doing U-turns. Coalition deputies were being dignified, but were clearly shattered. What could have gone wrong?

Late that night it was all wrapped up in North County Dublin. RTÉ had tea, sandwiches and some corrosive wine for its election workers. I dropped by on the way home. This Lucullan feast was in a radio studio, but as I approached the steps outside, Fianna Fáil leader Jack Lynch was emerging with his senior assistant and Press Officer, Frank Dunlop (yes, that Frank Dunlop). The RTÉ Director-General, Oliver Moloney, was approaching from Jack Lynch's left, his hand outstretched. The Fianna Fáil leader was a charismatic man with considerable charm – a kind of political Bing Crosby – but he could be vindictive. For reasons I never discovered, he chose to turn away from the Director-General, despite Frank Dunlop's best efforts, and withdrew to shake my hand instead. He greeted me by name and I mumbled my congratulations. Reluctantly, he turned and took the still-outstretched hand of Mr Moloney and then rushed off. I'm under no illusion that Jack Lynch thought I was more worthy of the attention. I was used as a calculated snub to the Director-General. Why? I don't know.

I learned a lot about elections in 1977 and have had a healthy distrust of pundits ever since. The politicians had made the same mistakes. They had got their arithmetic wrong, but their greatest error was not to listen to their constituents and to dismiss criticism as begrudgery or the utterance of a crank.

There was another lesson coming in 1979. The European elections were held against a background of rumbling discontent amongst Fianna Fáil back-benchers. There were too many of them and Lynch missed out on an opportunity to bring more bright new heads into government. I was assigned the election count in Kilkenny. The recently elected Albert Reynolds was the Fianna Fáil director of elections for Leinster – a formidable number-cruncher who did most of his calculations on the back of a Benson & Hedges cigarette box. But there was an even better tallyman there.

A plump young man with a Beatles haircut and brown pin-stripe suit was leaning over the barrier, watching the boxes being opened. He carried a pile of well-thumbed school jotters with lots of entries in pencil. Clearly he was comparing the figures in the jotters with his impressions of the newly opened ballot boxes. I asked him how it was going, and he immediately predicted a Fianna Fáil disaster. I wasn't going to file the forecast without detailed explanation. He said he was an accountant and the figures couldn't lie. He was also one of the new batch of Fianna Fáil deputies. His name was Charlie McCreevy and he was from Kildare. His jotters had ballot-box results from townlands and villages, cities and towns. The speed of his calculations was breathtaking. I'd boned up on election returns, but every time I raised a doubt about his forecast the jotters settled the matter.

I filed the copy and spoke to Gerald Barry in the RTÉ Newsroom. RTÉ is always on the lookout for good analysts and pundits at election time. I told him about young McCreevy, and it was Charlie's last election without a microphone nearby. The accuracy of his forecasts, both for Leinster and for the rest of the country, made him one of the best tallymen RTÉ ever had. He'll be missed. For McCreevy, the figures were the truth.

I've seen lots of elections since then, some of them close-run. There have been counts and re-counts that have gone on late, even into days. But if you ever want a rough guide to the possible outcome, you have to go local. When Ian Paisley took Terence O'Neill's Westminster seat, there was shock outside the constituency because no one had looked at their records within the constituency. O'Neill was a nice chap, Old Etonian, a bit embarrassed by his own party at times, and a poor constituency man. Paisley was a busy constituency worker, and all politics is local.

Brian Lenihan lost his Roscommon–Leitrim seat in 1973 because he spent too much time in Dublin. Ever after he preached the value of good constituency work and acute political hearing. When politicians listen only to their advisors, handlers and spin-doctors, it always ends in tears. The truth is out there and by election time, it's too late. People will give you their opinions, but you must ask first and then do what is most difficult for politicians of every hue: shut up and listen.

Most of us are in denial about something. Fat children used to be called 'big-boned' by their doting mothers. Believe me, I know. Others are 'regular social drinkers' when everyone else recognises them as alcoholics. Politicians stay in denial, but that denial becomes an act of faith within the party. The Labour party faithful believe they were punished at the ballot box because after the 'Spring Tide' of 1992 they went into coalition with Fianna Fáil. The fact is that two other events occurred before they were decimated at the polls. They brought down the Fianna Fáil government and they climbed into bed with Fine Gael.

Perhaps they should have examined their political promiscuity a bit more. Perhaps they also lost votes for bringing down a government, but this isn't countenanced by the party – at least, not publicly. The electoral preference for many would be a Fianna Fáil/Labour coalition. If the last such coalition was that bad, why would the public still want it? The personal relationships between Fianna Fáil and Labour ministers seemed more cordial than those between Fine Gael and Labour. There was no warmth between Dick Spring and John Bruton. They could do business, perhaps, but the public gave its verdict at the ballot box. By now, doctrinal and policy differences are clear between Labour, Fine Gael and the Green party, but we, the electorate, know that given a shot at government, these differences would be overcome – at any price. The differences between the Progressive Democrats and Fianna Fáil can irritate the back-benchers, but they too are set aside 'in the national interest'. Sinn Féin doesn't feature publicly as anyone's prospective coalition partners. The other parties are enthusiastic about Sinn Féin joining in government in Northern Ireland, but come out in hives at the prospect of it happening down here.

The ballot box is not the start of the electoral process, it's the opening of the final act. What happens before that will determine the outcome. A recent popular mayor of New Orleans, who later served time for corruption, declared accurately: 'The only way I won't be elected is if I'm found in bed with a dead girl or a live boy.'

An English politician seeking advice from an elder statesman asked about the dangers ahead. 'Events, dear boy, events!' Thus, as an election approaches the opposition will try to uncover or engineer as many events as possible. There is an ongoing debate about 'negative campaigning'. In the USA it has reached preposterous levels, with entirely fabricated scandals, slurs and doctored photographs. The law here doesn't permit that and opinion polls show that he who reaches for the first stone might only enhance the reputation of his target, at the expense of his own. The message is that any scandal would have to be monumental and undeniable to do any damage.

What's left? The government must defend its record, which it does with tedious regularity, and the opposition must attack that record, which it does, predictably, at any opportunity. It must also try to sell its own alternative policies, which it does poorly because they are not clear and coherent. The main battleground isn't, in fact, 'Morning Ireland', 'Questions and Answers' or even the floor of Dáil Éireann. It is the constituencies where local issues – hospitals, schools, transport and traffic – will have influence and, of course, 'events'. Did I say that all politics is local? It's more than that. It's personal.

Derek Davis joined RTÉ in 1974 and is a veteran of many elections on both sides of the border. In recent years he has delivered pre-election reports from around the country, giving the views of the citizen in the street. He currently contributes a regular column to 'Drivetime' on RTÉ Radio 1.

IX. Campaigns and Number-crunchers

Rodney Rice

Universities were different then. At least, I think they were. Certainly when I hear now that every UCD student who thinks there may be a subsequent advantage in being a member of Fianna Fáil piles into the Kevin Barry Cumann, it seems very different from the 1960s when I was studying at ... well, the Other Place.

But maybe that was just Trinity's way. No Charlie Haughey or Garret FitzGerald had ever passed through its portals, and no one from my year ended up in Cabinet. Although, in Mary Robinson we did produce an outstanding future President, of course. And a later TCD generation did deliver former PD leader and Tánaiste, current Minister for Health & Children, Mary Harney and her college debating society pal, one-time Fine Gael junior minister George Birmingham to Leinster House. Oh yes, and Dick Spring, another Tánaiste, who brought Labour to an historic high.

During my time, though, I don't remember any Fianna Fáil *cumann* nor a Fine Gael or Labour branch in college. Some, however, among that strange mix of English upper-classes, northern and southern Irish Protestant and increasingly southern Catholic middle-classes did take an interest in the politics of the State outside Front Square. That's how I got my first taste of a general election. Seán Lemass had dissolved the Dáil for an April 1965 poll. A couple of casual friends from (let's be honest) O'Neill's Bar in Dublin's Suffolk Street invited me to canvass for a young Labour party hopeful, the late Michael O'Leary, who was carrying the terrible cross of being a Corkman seeking election in Dublin North Central.

The instructions were simple: don't mention Cork, and if a voter did, stress the handsome young candidate's trade union work in his adopted city. If in doubt, hit home with the story that the other Labour candidate was a wealthy solicitor who was also a landlord. That should be a telling point in the working-class streets of the North Inner City.

And who knows, perhaps it was. O'Leary won by a handful of votes on the thirteenth count, defeating his party colleague. So I learned an important practical lesson about the Single Transferable Vote system: your most dangerous rival may well be your party ticket partner. That new-found knowledge has proven to be of constant value in all my subsequent electoral involvement as an RTÉ journalist since the very next election, that of June 1969.

Then a youthful reporter on the television current affairs programme '7Days', I was at the Bolton Street count-centre to relay to the audience the comments of politicians watching nervously to see if they were to be part of a re-elected Fianna Fáil, a resurgent Fine Gael, or a standard-bearer for the Labour party's audacious claim that the 'Seventies will be Socialist'.

Frank Cluskey, later to be Labour's leader, was not amused by my forceful questioning in a live interview to have him admit that the tail-end of the 1960s was showing no signs of heralding a socialist Ireland. We had become reasonably friendly, amused by an instinctive interaction of edgy and mordant repartee. 'That'll teach me not to treat journalists as friends,' he said drily after that interview.

I was not, however, the tyro journo who, in 1981, when Frank lost his seat, aimed his microphone at him and asked, 'Mr Cluskey, to what do ascribe your defeat?' 'I didn't get enough votes,' responded Frank.

Before those tense political days of the early 1980s, when the country faced three general elections in eighteen months, we had the campaigns of 1973 and 1977. The former saw Fine Gael and Labour enter it with an agreed programme for government, and the people returned the first coalition government since Fianna Fáil had recaptured power in 1957.

On election night 1973 I was in the count-centre for Dún Laoghaire-Rathdown, the constituency of Fine Gael leader Liam Cosgrave. Even though a change of government was clear to our studio pundits, I could not persuade him in our interview to agree that his hour to become Taoiseach had arrived.

Liam Cosgrave was a cautious man with the media, and I recall, when he was well retired, conducting careful negotiations with him by letter of invitation and then face-to-face discussions before he would to contribute to a programme I was compiling on the fiftieth anniversary of the founding of Fine Gael. Eventually he came into the RTÉ radio centre for the recording. He told me it was the first time he had ever been in the building, even though it had been RTÉ Radio headquarters since halfway through his period in power. Afterwards, I asked him if he would talk to me in greater detail about his period as Taoiseach. 'No,' he replied, 'I think I have said enough.' So RTÉ's Sound Archive is pretty light on the reflections of this former leader.

There will be much more in the archives of the voice of Cosgrave's successor, Jack Lynch, who returned to power in the great giveaway of 1977. That year I was in studio, co-presenting the results programme with Kevin Healy. Amazingly, party strategist Martin O'Donoghue still defends the Fianna Fáil overheating manifesto he is credited with having developed, which promised to abolish house rates and car road tax. It was a surefire winner coming after the oil crisis-created hair-shirt years, which had inspired 'Hall's Pictorial Weekly' on RTÉ Television to reinvent Minister for Finance Richie Ryan as 'Richie Ruin, the Minister for Hardship'.

The most memorable moments of our radio coverage that night came with the remarkably prescient 7.00pm prediction from Gerald Barry, who was crunching the numbers so far available, that Fianna Fáil would be returned with a landslide of at least eighty-two of the 148 seats. Later, when party leader Jack Lynch was told that the likely outcome now was that he would have eighty-four seats, he replied to us: 'I hope not.'

The perceptiveness of that comment became clear just two years later, when that lumbering mass of back-benchers for whom no Office of State could be found proved willing supporters of the resurgent Charlie Haughey, who had chewed the chicken in each of their constituencies and now moved against the man who had sacked him during the Arms Crisis of 1970. Two by-elections lost in 1979 and it was goodbye to 'Honest Jack'.

The scene was set for those epic Haughey/FitzGerald clashes. The Garret FitzGerald-led Fine Gael won in June 1981, but lost power the following January after a Budget proposal to charge VAT on shoes.

'How can families afford VAT on children's shoes?' went one cry. 'Exclude children's shoes.'

'But what about well-heeled ladies with small feet?' came another voice. From memory, it belonged to the late George Colley, perhaps not serving his party as well as his nemesis, party leader Haughey, would have desired. Fianna Fáil took to the saddle again after a bruising contest.

Three vignettes from that election. Garret's enduring fascination with transport brought those of us who were reporting on his campaign to Connolly Station in Dublin one morning, with our toothbrushes packed for a Magical Mystery Tour. The special train went via Mayo, for a spot of hand-shaking, to Galway and on to Limerick, in part using track re-opened for the day by CIÉ. It's great what you can swing when you have the power.

Michael O'Leary, Labour leader and outgoing Tánaiste, also used his power, albeit in a minor way. Visiting a school in Tarbert, in North Kerry, the headmaster's delight faded when the Tánaiste announced a half-day for the pupils.

The students cheered in delight and there was no going back. The problem for their headmaster was that the school buses were not due until the customary afternoon pick-up time. He was left with responsibility for a school body granted freedom from learning, but with nowhere to go. What can a Tánaiste do? Dash on at speed to the next port of call, of course. And hope his two accompanying journalists did not pick up on the problem he had caused.

No chance. O'Leary was on borrowed time with us already. I had met Maev Kennedy of *The Irish Times* the previous evening at the Shannon Airport Hotel. The restaurant was closed, and all of the bar food available included smoked salmon: smoked salmon salad, smoked salmon sandwich, smoked salmon roll ... We went out for greater sustenance, but found only fish and chips.

On our return we sought out the Labour leader in his room. He was on the telephone and his colleague, the late Senator Michael Ferris, chatted to us in the corridor. Strangely, he began manoeuvring us around, keeping our backs at all times to an approaching waiter. Maev glanced back.

'What's that, Mick? Smoked salmon?'

'No, it's ham.'

'It's smoked salmon, Mick.'

'Ham. Ham.'

'Mick,' I protested, 'the only thing they sell here is smoked salmon.'

'It's fucking ham,' he roared, still attempting to keep our eyes averted.

It was a time when it was the height of insult to call a Labour member a 'smoked salmon socialist'. And there was no better candidate for that sobriquet than the former baiter of Labour's tiny landlord class, the bould O'Leary. Maev and I agreed to let that one go. But the half-day off to be spent in the Tarbert schoolyard was too good to ignore.

When the count was in, the coalition had lost. Fianna Fáil returned with an unstable support base of Independents and Workers party deputies. It was not long before that government fell, and we took to the road again.

Every political journalist has his or her fund of Haughey stories, almost inevitably centring on abuse being heaped upon their heads by the Squire of Kinsealy. During this campaign, outgoing Taoiseach FitzGerald had a meeting with a British aristocrat and an all-Ireland policing solution was mentioned. Charlie went on the warpath. But listening to him in Cahirciveen, I sensed that his threat that it would lead to B-Specials on the local streets was creating less than startled fear and uncontrolled outrage among the populace. On the way to Millstreet, I joined the Fianna Fáil leader in his car for a campaign trail interview.

He repeated his anger at the FitzGerald suggestion.

'But, Mr Haughey,' I pressed, 'you're the one who talks about looking at the totality of relationships between our islands.'

Full thirty seconds of silence followed. Only when Haughey, who was sitting in the front seat, heard the click of my recording being stopped did he turn to me.

'Listen, Mr Rodney-fucking-Rice. If you think I'm going to be interrogated by a c— like you ...'

The car stopped abruptly in the middle of Millstreet and Haughey alighted and headed for a makeshift stage, where his party's three candidates awaited him. He commended each of them by name to the small crowd. But as with Eric Morecambe's reply to orchestra conductor André Previn's claim that he had played all the wrong notes, Mr Haughey used all the right names, but not necessarily in the right order. Mr X was Mr Y, Mr Y was Mr Z and Mr Z was Mr X. He left the platform quickly, his candidates less than flattered, and returned to the car. He glowered at me and said, 'Get in and see do we get on better this time.' Same questions, but he had thought of some answers.

To think it had been only a little more than a year since Haughey had extended a genial invitation to me and a colleague to join him in a bottle of his favourite Château Lynch-Bages, during the previous election campaign in Letterkenny, County Donegal. I wonder now who was paying for that?

After that November 1982 election, Haughey faced almost five years in opposition, and halfway through that tried to sabotage the newly negotiated Anglo-Irish Agreement, then later expelled Des O'Malley from Fianna Fáil, which led to the foundation of the Progressive Democrats.

The new party provided the story of the 1987 election. In spite of unpropitious economic circumstances and the departure of Labour from the outgoing coalition, election night saw fourteen Progressive Democrats returned, including eight newcomers to the Dáil. Although the first PDs had been defectors from Fianna Fáil, many of their first-time voters were people Fine Gael had hoped to rely on, which meant the latter party sustained the heaviest losses. Even then, however, Charlie Haughey needed the abstention of Tony Gregory and the casting vote of Ceann Comhairle Sean Treacy to see him back in Office for the third time.

That was another Haughey government that was unlikely to last a full term, and in 1989 it fell after losing a vote to provide IR£400,000 to help haemophiliacs cruelly infected with HIV. It was an unnecessary defeat, but the Taoiseach had just returned, tired, from Japan and someone said he had learned there that respect was shown by how deep one bowed to a superior. Some deputy had not bowed low enough towards the Great Leader.

Election night in studio had been tense and exciting as those of us at the statistics table, which I now chaired each count night, reported four Fianna Fáil and eight PD losses. But the real drama came when, after two failed attempts to elect a Taoiseach, at the third time of asking the Dáil was presented with the first coalition government in which Fianna Fáil had ever been involved. Charles J Haughey's need for power forced him to bite his lip hard and bow towards a partnership with his old enemy, Des O'Malley, and his Progressive Democrats.

Three years later we were on the trail again. Haughey was gone – victim to a claim on television, by former Justice Minister Seán Doherty, that the leader had known in the early 1980s that the phones of two journalists were being tapped.

Albert Reynolds succeeded him as leader of Fianna Fáil, but he and Des O'Malley fell out over Beef Tribunal claims and a dispirited Fianna Fáil team took to the trail, where it was claimed no one wanted to meet them.

One memory that may be symptomatic of that feeling of defeatism was a press conference where the outgoing Minister for Finance, Bertie Ahern, presented his financial manifesto. I did a back-of-the-envelope costing of proposed tax changes and asked the Minister about them. The answer failed to satisfy at least one journalist who, as Mr Ahern was preparing to leave, asked him again about these costs. 'Ask Rodney. He's done the figures,' was the reply. Even today, only Bertie could get away with that.

The 'Spring Tide' was on the way. An historic thirty-three seats for Dick Spring's Labour party was more than any of us had foreseen. Equally surprising was Labour's decision to join Fianna Fáil in coalition for the first time ever after the new Dáil had met three times without producing a Taoiseach or government.

Clerical sex abuse and poor internal communications brought that experiment to a premature end, of course. But what really annoyed us political groupies – whatever about the Plain People of Ireland – was being cheated out of a campaign and another exciting late night at the studio. For the first time, a new government was formed from within the Dáil, without an election. Hmmpph!

We had better luck in 1997 when, with a new and more confident Ireland burgeoning forth and showing early shoots of growing wealth, we might have thought the Rainbow coalition could achieve electoral vindication.

But no. Labour got well and truly thrashed, either for having gone in with Fianna Fáil in the first place or for having left them prematurely. The old certainties re-established themselves: Fianna

Fáil and Fine Gael made substantial gains, and the only choices of government were a renewed Fianna Fáil/Labour pledge or a Fianna Fáil/Progressive Democrats pact, with support from the Independents.

That's the excitement of elections. For at least some of us, getting it wrong initially is better fun along the way than predicting the predictable from the outset.

Bertie Ahern and Mary Harney came to power, assisted by the Fianna Fáil gene pool, and in 2002 their partnership produced the first government to be returned since 1969.

These past forty years that these recollections have quickly spanned have changed Ireland totally, of course. We have near full employment, immigration to replace emigration and a national income we could scarcely have imagined. Electorally, however, we have a remarkable consistency. So I summarise here what I have observed.

For all that Fine Gael's representation dropped in 2002 to just one more than its lowest ever total – and that in a smaller Dáil in 1944 – the party remains, with Fianna Fáil, the core vote-catcher of our system. Labour continues fluctuating, but unchallenged yet in third place.

Fine Gael is historically the party of the Big House, the large farmer, the comfortable shopkeeper. The party has seen a not-insignificant number of such people become the floating voters, perhaps motivated by a very clear perception of self-interest. Many are attracted to the low tax, private service provision policies best represented by the Progressive Democrats.

The PDs opted for an ideology that would differentiate them from the Fianna Fáil party their founders had left, an unattributed Thatcherism or Reaganomics that is now better known as neo-liberalism. It seems to me that the crucial backing they got came from Fianna Fáil Minister for Finance, Charlie McCreevy.

Such policies did not, however, become the manifesto fare of Fianna Fáil, whose leader opted to proclaim himself a socialist in the knowledge that Fianna Fáil and Labour compete for the allegiance of the smaller farmer and the urban working class. The history of nationalism in Ireland puts the former party well ahead of Labour in the contest for this support, even though Fianna Fáil seems these days to prefer to send out a mixed, but ideology-free message, supporting property developers in their projects while protecting social welfare and pension rates.

What we did see in 2002 was an increase in the number of Independents and the multiplying in size of the Sinn Féin representation. Clearly this growing splintering of the vote produces surprise results in individual constituencies, with single-issue candidates and flavour-of-the-month smaller parties seeing their elected numbers expand and condense unpredictably.

So in 2007 the ups and downs of the three major parties will be deeply affected by the unclear fortunes of Sinn Féin, the usually unpredictable challenge of the Independents and the rise or fall of the Progressive Democrats and the Green party. And that's what will keep RTÉ's daily radio coverage – on the stump, in the studio and on election night – so engrossing for a people who can't stop loving and hating politicians.

For me, this should be my final election before retirement. But as the man could have said: 'Three years is a long time in politics.'

Rodney Rice is one of RTÉ's most senior current affairs presenters. Since the mid-1980s he has presented 'Saturday View' and 'Worlds Apart' on RTÉ Radio 1. He has played a senior role in election coverage both in the Republic and in Northern Ireland, and this year anchored RTÉ Radio coverage of the Northern Assembly elections.

X. Polls, parties and papers

Gerald Barry

> *'It ain't what they say, it's the way that they say it'*

> 'Opinion polls are not predictive of events that might be weeks or months away.'
>
> 'They are snapshots in time.'
>
> 'They are accurate within a known statistical margin of error – even when different surveys taken within the same statistical universe at an identical or similar time produce different results.'

These are frequent refrains from those who produce the market surveys, although they get less prominence than used, perhaps, be the case. They are reasonable assertions. Furthermore, neither sample selection nor question formulation ever appear to be tainted by bias or political prejudice. Yet there are reasons to cast a colder eye on their presentation, both by those who commission and release the results and by those in charge of their assembly and collation.

For the purposes of this contribution, the figures, reporting and commentaries (unless otherwise stated) refer to the tns/MRBI surveys for *The Irish Times*, published in December 2006 and February 2007.

From their earliest production in the mid-1970s – when the results were known mainly to political parties with the requisite financial clout, who were also more perceptive than the media about their potential usefulness – most polling companies said they believed their final pre-election polls were reasonably, and sometimes very, close to actual election outcomes.

To take a small number of slightly contrasting examples. In 1977, in what is still widely regarded as the biggest election upset in relatively recent Irish history, the outgoing Fine Gael/Labour government was defeated as Fianna Fáil was restored to office with a big overall majority – the last occasion on which it has achieved that objective. With virtual unanimity the political media had predicted a return of the Fine Gael/Labour coalition. A small number of people knew otherwise. Fine Gael (who shared their knowledge with the Labour leaders) and Fianna Fáil knew from their respective pollsters – MRBI and IMS – that final pre-voting polls had Fianna Fáil on 51 per cent. That would, and did, produce a clear overall majority. The final pre-election polls had proved extremely accurate.

Those were private polls, the results available only to the purchasers. By the time of the next general election, in June 1981, the situation had changed.

The *Irish Independent* commissioned MRBI to execute the first publicly available political opinion poll. It was carried out one week before polling day. Having excluded the 'don't knows' and adjusted party support levels proportionately, they found the levels of support for the main parties to be as follows: Fianna Fáil, 45 per cent; Fine Gael, 38 per cent; Labour, 11 per cent; and Others, 6 per cent.

When the votes were counted, Fianna Fáil got exactly that percentage; Fine Gael and Labour got just 1 per cent less than predicted; while Others received 2 per cent more.

By the time of the November 1982 election, the third during this period, MRBI's expertise had been purchased by *The Irish Times*.

The final pre-election figures produced by the company and published in the newspaper were again very close to the actual outcome: Fianna Fáil got an extra 1 per cent in real voting support, Fine Gael 2 per cent less and Labour the identical amount.

In the five elections since then, the final MRBI/*Irish Times* poll has always overestimated the final Fianna Fáil actual first-preference vote by an average of more than 3 per cent; underestimated the Fine Gael vote by an average of a bit more than 1 per cent; and been quite close to the actual Labour performance.

Since 1997 the polling organisation has made changes to its sampling techniques, its post-polling calculations and its presentation of results to take account of these perceived difficulties. *The Irish Times'* presentation of the results has also altered considerably.

There has been little public debate about what has been involved and about the nature of these changes. In the published data there has been no regular information explaining what are substantial changes side by side with the results. The accompanying tns/MRBI commentary goes off on a completely different course.

All of this is very surprising given that some serious questions seem to arise. This chapter seeks to raise some of these questions; definitive answers will require more information and greater technical expertise.

Probably the most serious questions arise in relation to the presentation of the area given greatest prominence both by the pollsters and by the newspaper in its lead stories, front-page graphics and editorial analysis. This involves the so-called adjusted level of party support. There is little or no ongoing information as to the necessity for the 'adjustment' nor explanation as to how it has been calculated. It would be easy to assume, in these absences, that this comprises what those surveyed have actually said once their answers have been compiled properly.

It does not.

Any misapprehension is then compounded on the inside page where more details are printed. A 'strap' headline contains a question: 'If there were a general election tomorrow, to which party would you give your first-preference vote?'

Underneath this is a graphic indicating support levels for the main parties/groups. The linkage here is even more direct. It suggests that this graphic consists of the tallied totals of responses by those surveyed to the above question.

It does not.

Two important changes (or, at least, two that are of interest here) have been made to the original data. First, 'don't know/no opinion' answers have been excluded, which allows for the fact that not everyone votes, and does not alter the *relative* support for the different parties. In addition, the polling company has made its 'adjustment' – a calculation apparently based on its final poll overestimation of what later turned out to be the actual Fianna Fáil first-preference vote and its underestimation of the actual Fine Gael vote in the immediately preceding general elections.

None of this is mentioned or explained, however. In particular, neither the fact of nor the detailed reasoning behind the 'adjustment'.

It is not the case that this basic information is not available or is not included. It is there, but you have to look for it. It is the smallest of the tables, and it is not presented as the actual answer to the question at the top of the page. This is labelled the 'core' support and differs substantially from the 'adjusted' support.

From this 'core' vote, through the vote excluding those who do not indicate a party or group preference and to the 'adjusted' the following are the major changes which have taken place. (The figures underneath come from the survey reported in *The Irish Times*, 2 February 2007.)

Fianna Fáil's support rises by 8 per cent from 'core' to the second category, and is then reduced by 6 per cent for its final 'adjusted' level, which is the headline figure used by tns/MRBI and by *The Irish Times*.

Every party increases from 'core' to 'don't know' category except, in this latest poll, the Progressive Democrats, whose total support was so tiny. Every party, other than Fianna Fáil and the PDs, sees its vote adjusted upwards. From 'core' through to 'adjusted' Fine Gael rises from its 'core' of 19 per cent to 26 per cent (a base rate increase of 37 per cent), while Labour increases from 8 per cent to 11 per cent (a base rate increase of 38 per cent).

All of this, it seems, is because on a number of occasions the final election poll differed from the polling-day result. Should we conclude that the earlier polls had some defect in them, even that they were 'wrong'?

Are they wrong now? Is there any scientific reason for saying that, since opinion poll data differed from subsequent election results, all future surveys have to be 'adjusted'? Opinion polls were not meant to be predictive, were they?

The changes involved are quite substantial. They may be warranted. They may give a truer picture. I don't know. I cannot know because there is no explanation, let alone a detailed one. The same must be true for practically all readers of *The Irish Times*.

One thing is clear: the final figures are not a direct representation of the views stated by those surveyed. They are calculations, based on previous results and election outcomes, of the polling organisation's belief as to the *meaning* of what their sample actually told them.

If previous polls which did not use these techniques were wrong, why and by how much did they err? Were any such errors outside the normal plus or minus 3 per cent for each individual figure? If the changes had been made because of differences in final pre-election polls when compared to actual election outcomes, why are adjustments made to party support levels in intervening polls? In intervening polls (i.e. ones not immediately followed by an election), how can the polling organisation know an adjustment is necessary and the scale of such in the absence of any adjacent yardstick by which it can be measured?

There are other puzzling issues.

When those sampled are asked about their levels of satisfaction/dissatisfaction in relation to government performance, the response parameters are different. By this I mean that there is a noticeable difference between, say, the satisfaction levels with government and the declared intention to vote for either of the two parties currently in government. In five *Irish Times'* polls since the beginning of 2006 the satisfaction level exceeds the adjusted party support by about 7 per cent, on average.

There are a number of reasons why this could be so. Could *one* of them be that there is no 'adjustment' (along the lines used for party support levels) made to the 'satisfaction' figures?

There is some – far from conclusive – evidence to bolster consideration of such an effect. It comes again from *The Irish Times* survey published in the first week of February 2007.

On 'day one' of their three-day presentation of the results (Friday, 2 February), the page-one lead story said that the 'alternative coalitions are polling neck and neck'. This was based on the tns/MRBI 'adjusted' party support figures. The alternative coalitions being referred to are Fianna Fáil and the PDs on the one side, Fine Gael and Labour on the other. In the leading article of that day's *Irish Times* the following is stated: 'support for Fine Gael, Labour and the Green party has placed them in a commanding position.' The editorial goes on to warn the main opposition against reading too much into the latest data. Coverage of new data from the poll (in addition to the first-day figures) is included. The question asked is: which of these possible coalitions would you like to form the next government?

Three possible coalition alternatives were shown to each voter: Fianna Fáil and the Progressive Democrats; Fine Gael, Labour and the Green party; Fianna Fáil and the Labour party. In that order the figures ascertained were: 32 per cent, 29 per cent and 13 per cent. Since neither filtering nor 'adjustment' has occurred, the data also threw up figures of 12 per cent for 'none of these' and 14 per cent for 'don't know'.

Comparisons with the paper's previous poll are difficult because a similar question relating to the third (FF/Lab) alternative was excluded. It might still be reasonable to assume that support for any government featuring Fianna Fáil had probably dropped, because of a decrease in the Fianna Fáil core vote.

Perhaps what is of most interest in these non-adjusted figures is that support for the main alternative coalition – the only alternative even partially on offer – is also lower. This figure is also adversely affected by the addition of a (not-on-offer) coalition.

Fewer than three out of every ten people surveyed opted for the current main opposition alternative. Arising from those responses, you would be hard pressed to describe them as depicting a 'commanding position'.

Opinion polls are extraordinarily useful and can be exceptionally powerful tools. Journalists (such as myself), political parties and academics all find them a crucial part of their activities. There are other, wider areas worth discussing. But surely it is right that polls, their compilation, analysis and conclusions, should be subject to rigorous scrutiny and debate.

Gerald Barry is the editor and a presenter of 'This Week' on RTÉ Radio 1 each Sunday at lunchtime. A programme that, in the wake of election results, often opens the debate on the options for government. He has been involved in election coverage since the general election of 1973. He is a former Political Correspondent of the *Sunday Tribune*.

XI. Passing time in the Seanad

David Davin-Power

The plight of the candidate seeking election to the Seanad is perhaps unique in the western political world. Securing a nomination from one of the range of bodies – some of which have the most tenuous connections with the world of politics – is bad enough; the aspirant senator must then trudge the byways seeking the approval of an electorate that is shrewd, highly politicised, deeply partisan and occasionally vindictive.

Consider the high-profile candidate some years ago who spent an afternoon attempting to convince one councillor to back him. After prolonged argument, success seemed assured. All the more so when an offer was made to mark the ballot paper there and then; surely no vote was ever more copperfastened? The mark was made, an additional flourish the use of a distinctive pen. Imagine the chagrin of our hero when, ruefully surveying a less-than-impressive pile of papers at the count some weeks later, he spies the ballot paper in question; surely here, at least, is a number one? But, alas, closer inspection revealed the depth of treachery of which the electorate in the Upper House is sometimes capable: a 3 had been appended to the 1. Even in Seanad elections a thirteenth preference is rarely much use.

If you do get returned, in time you will enter a chamber where debate can be less constrained and more unpredictable than proceedings downstairs in the Dáil. One order of business in recent times heard a sequence of contributions that was more a stream of consciousness, as members ranged in short order over insurance costs, the war in Iraq, suicide prevention at home, the merits of Dublin GAA club Clan na Gael Fontenoy, The Battle of Fontenoy, the poem inspired by that encounter, the evils of urban incinerators and airport policy.

This five-minute flight of fancy was capped with a quote from Goldsmith's 'The Deserted Village', a location to which the chamber's press gallery frequently bears more than a passing resemblance. The current leader of the house was heard to commend one journalist on finding his way there; it must also be recorded that one of the longest-serving correspondents in Leinster House recently conceded that he had not graced the Seanad's portals since 1981.

The pace of business in the Seanad is scarcely frenetic. One former member recalls a colleague struggling to make up his allotted time in a debate. He seized, as a rhetorical device, a small scrap of plaster that was floating gently down a sunbeam from the chamber's elegant stuccoed ceiling. He mused in general terms about what such an insignificant mote might tell us about the broader argument ... for instance, could it point to some deeper deficiency? On a practical note, he suggested jocosely, maybe the ceiling needed to be looked at. The literal-minded Board of Works took him at his word, and uncovered a state of affairs that prompted a multi-million-euro repair job.

The House can, of course, tease out government policy at greater length and in a more discursive way than the Dáil. Most ministers prefer the relaxed ambience in what was once the Leinster House ballroom. Useful amendments and the odd piece of legislation have been introduced here. There is, however, a general agreement that the House needs reform, and an equally widely held view that procedures are likely to remain unchanged for the foreseeable future.

Those entitled to vote in elections comprise some 1,000 city and county councillors, outgoing senators and members of the incoming Dáil. The original intention was that the Upper House might reflect the wider social economy, with members elected to so-called vocational panels. The framers of the Constitution might have hoped for a more independent chamber, but there is no disguising the fact that in recent years it has been used increasingly by the parties as an incubator for TDs, as well as a decompression chamber for those licking their wounds after unsuccessful Dáil campaigns.

Five years ago even well-respected, long-term senators, like Fine Gael's Maurice Manning, now Head of the Human Rights Commission, were axed by a party that wanted to focus on candidates whose eyes were fixed on the eventual prize of a Dáil seat. That is a tendency that is unlikely to be reversed, and one that has played to the advantage of so-called independent senators, who are elected to the two university panels. Untrammelled by party considerations, they are free to roam across the day's political agenda. Glance at the Seanad monitor, at the order of business, and more likely than not either David Norris, Shane Ross, or Joe O'Toole will be on their feet. Their position gives the independents a unique perspective on the workings of the Upper House and on Seanad reform – a perennial political aspiration to rival draining the Shannon.

Joe O'Toole believes there is nothing inherently wrong with having councillors involved in elections to the chamber, but that rather the problem lies in the dominance they exert over the system. However, he regards the university panels, to which he is elected, as indefensible and undemocratic, but insists that meaningful reforms need not involve further constitutional change.

Some, like Taoiseach's nominee Maurice Hayes, believe that change should be less ambitious and start with the way the Seanad orders its business. 'There are plenty of reports that need discussion in the more relaxed way in which we can consider issues,' he says, deploring the practice of having the House exchange statements on issues of the day as useless time-filling.

But the latest set of proposals for reform of the Upper House are now three years old, and as likely to be implemented as any of their predecessors. In 2004 an all-party committee recommended scrapping the vocational panels and radically changing the method of election. Twenty-six of the proposed sixty-five places would be elected directly to a new national constituency at the same time as local and European polls; another twenty would be returned by councillors and Oireachtas members in the wake of Dáil elections, as at present; and the anomaly whereby only graduates of the National University of Ireland and Trinity College, Dublin, can elect university members would be ended.

An implementation group has been considering the proposals since then, but no one is holding their breath. Indeed, one measure of the urgency that attaches to Seanad reform can be seen in the fact that the constitutional amendment, backed by the people nearly thirty years ago, to extend the university franchise has never been implemented. Like the PD policy of abolishing the Seanad, it has been quietly shelved.

The reason? The broad range of elements whose interests are served by keeping things as they are. The main parties have clearly shown their hand by packing the current house with members who have Dáil aspirations. They are content to leave the Seanad as a forum for grooming future TDs.

The government, which directly nominates eleven members, has no appetite for giving up a vital piece of patronage. Senators themselves have an influential role in deciding who will succeed them. The university members have the best of all possible worlds: a good salary, a downtown office, no real political obligations beyond securing their own re-election and, above all, no requirement to hang around for votes.

The election of Sinn Féin or Green senators might alter the tone of the Seanad, but it has so far shown an impressive ability to embrace even those whose stated aim was its abolition – as the Progressive Democrats have discovered. As things stand, there seems little prospect of substantial change in this worthy, self-perpetuating and ultimately undervalued institution.

David Davin-Power is Political Editor with RTÉ News. Working across radio and television news programmes, he and the political correspondents and reporters will provide a vital insight for the audience in the run-up to Election 2007. Prior to his appointment in Dublin, he was RTÉ Northern Editor in Belfast.

XII. 'What's this scam all about?' (or how Mountjoy prison is preparing for the prisoners' first ballot)

Áine Lawlor

On average, 3,500 prisoners are held in Irish prisons each day. This has been a fairly consistent average over the past seven-odd years. Seven to eight hundred of those incarcerated are held in Mountjoy prison, in Dublin. This year, for the first time, eligible citizens held in Irish prisons will have the right to vote in the general election. Mountjoy prison Governor, John Lonergan, welcomes this development. He says it should have been done years ago. He agreed to our request to come into the prison in early February to talk to him and the inmates about the right to vote, the practicalities involved, what it means to the prisoners and the issues that matter to them in the election.

The prison itself was built in 1846. Then it was called Her Majesty's Model Prison. There's little model about Mountjoy these days. It is widely accepted that the prison is old and overcrowded, and unfit for the demands and standards of the twenty-first century. The Inspector of Prisons has severely criticised conditions there in several reports. The current Minister for Justice, Michael McDowell, plans a new prison at Thornton Hall in place of Mountjoy, moving its landmark presence away from Dublin city centre and out into the north of the county.

As we walk through its gates, the first impression is that we have walked onto the set of the TV series 'Porridge'. It looks just the same: the grey stonework, the clanging steel gates and, inside, the corridors with their Victorian ironwork, the fenced-off landings

121

above us and, hanging in the air, the smell of bleach. An incongruous reminder of the twenty-first century is the handprint reader the prison officers use several times for identification purposes as they unlock and re-lock the several sets of gates we walk through.

First, we meet Governor Lonergan, who explains how prison voting will work. At this stage he has two forms to distribute to the prisoners. The first is an application to be placed on the electoral register; as he points out, many of the inmates will not have voted before. The second form is an application for a postal vote, as this is the system chosen for the prison ballot. The majority of Mountjoy's inmates are from the city itself: up to 80 per cent are Dublin-based. However, Governor Lonergan points out that they are dealing with up to seven or eight constituencies, and that's before you take into consideration those from outside Dublin. Nobody seems quite sure yet how interested the various political parties will be in trying to canvass the Mountjoy electorate.

The big problem is that by the time the election takes place, in the summer, perhaps May, those who do actually go through the process of filling out those forms could have been transferred to other prisons, or have been released. At this stage there is no way to know who will be where then. The other reality the Governor acknowledges is the lack of interest so far.

Despite all this, John Lonergan is adamant that the prison ballot is a positive development. He talks passionately about the prisoners' rights as citizens, like everyone on the outside, to exercise their vote. He seems rueful, realistic and oddly optimistic. We talk again about the terms we have agreed for the visit: we will be taken around the workshops, it will be up to the men themselves whether they talk to us and we will not identify the individuals we speak to by name. So we leave our teacups in the Governor's office and proceed to the workshops, accompanied by the clanging of gates and the clanking of keys.

On our way down we walk past the visiting area. You can see straight in, to quite a small, modern, concrete block room, with seats on either side of a chest-high partition and prison officers at the end. A few families are on one side; their fathers on the left. It feels like an intrusion to be looking in, probably because of the desperate edge to the big smiles on the men's faces as they look over the partition at their children. We hear that there is a generation of women who have visited their sons here who are now visiting their grandsons, and of men receiving visits from the different mothers of their various children. There is also the fear that a child who grows up coming in through those gates on family visits is more likely to end up here as an adult.

Then we are through into the workshops, where the atmosphere is busy and seems cheerful. Perhaps it's the novelty of two women journalists – I am with my colleague from 'Morning Ireland', Emer Lowe – but most of the men we meet this morning have plenty to say, if not about the election, then certainly about some of the issues that are likely to be debated during the campaign, such as crime, punishment and drugs. The fact that they have the right to vote is news to most, though, and initially the reaction is one of apathy and downright suspicion.

One man in his twenties, Séan we'll call him, sums it up like this: 'What's this scam all about anyway?' He has seen a notice about it on the landing, but he reckons it has to be a scam, that there has to be someone or something behind it. After all, he argues, who wants to give criminals the vote and why do they want to do it now? We explain, but he's still not sure. Who's behind this and why now?

Many of the guys can't read or write, is someone trying to scam their vote? Will the ballot be as private for them as everyone else? Nothing he's told by us or his fellow inmates can shift his suspicion that someone has an ulterior motive in this whole exercise and is not to be trusted. It dawns on me for the first, but not the last, time this morning that these are men who know that the rest of us look at them only to look away, that we fear and distrust them, and they carry that sense of being outside the loop of common concern in our society. Several of the men we meet refer to themselves in passing as scumbags.

Only one man we encounter has any sense of himself as a citizen of Ireland, with a right to vote and have a say in choosing the next government. Tony talks passionately and at length, exhorting his fellow inmates to have their say in the election, and perhaps they could help to put prison reform on the political agenda.

Suddenly they all want to talk. By this time it's clear that most of the men we're talking to are, or have been, drug addicts. It's the recurring riff in everyone's conversation. Drugs. Do we know there's not enough rehab, not enough therapy? Do we know that even if you get yourself clean when you're inside, on the outside there are long delays when you look for places on maintenance programmes and for housing? So that what happens next is they go back on drugs, they get back into crime and they're back inside.

Tony chips in again. He says the way the prison system works at the moment, it's designed to make them re-offend. He argues that the only way to really cut crime figures is to invest in more drug therapy, counselling, education and rehabilitation, with better link-ups with the outside world on discharge so that they can stay on the straight and narrow. He's really impressing us all, but then he starts to talk about the fact that heroin is not as bad for you as alcohol, and I realise he's probably got a habit as well. Tony says Ireland should decriminalise drugs if we want to break the link between drugs and crime.

I ask about mandatory prison sentences for drugs offences, and again this provokes a big reaction from the group that have gathered around us. They are all aware of Michael McDowell's stand on the issue, and they all disagree with him. Only the judges understand what's going on they say, and they'd rather trust the judges than Michael McDowell. One man says the judges are probably being a bit soft, but it's only the mules they say, the lower-level drug addicts who are just trying to feed their habits, who are ending up in court. Several of the men compare the length of sentences being doled out for drugs offences with the lesser sentences they say paedophiles get. Besides that, we're told, it's not the big drug dealers who are getting caught and they're not the ones who are facing mandatory sentences.

So, what can be done about the increase in drug-fuelled gun crime? One guy just back from an English prison says we 'ain't seen nothing yet'. It will get worse, he says. At the moment it's coke and guns, soon it will be crack and guns and the murder rate will rise even higher. We're almost laughed at for asking a question that imagines this can be made better. Nothing will change. The gang bosses are only interested in money, one man in the carpentry workshop tells us. Drugs and guns are their business and they'll go on doing what they do to make money. The idea that any politician, or any government, or any election can make any difference to that fact is just ridiculous. They don't care about innocent people. They don't care what laws are passed nor what sentences handed down in courts. It's bad, it's been made worse by coke, and it will get worse again.

He's not so sure either that more drug therapy or counselling would make much of a difference to himself and the other guys in Mountjoy. By the time they end up here, he says, it's too late. If you want to make a difference, you'd need to step in earlier, he says, St Patrick's – the institution for young offenders – even earlier ... he doesn't tell us at what time in his or anyone else's life anyone could have made a difference.

We are approached by one man who wants to talk about immigration. He thinks that's an election issue, even though he has been behind bars here in the prison for the past five years. He's heard, he's been told that it's a big problem out there. Immigrants are taking over 'our' housing, 'our' jobs' and 'our' schools. The government should do more to stop them. He's not sure that he will vote, but if he did vote, immigration would be an important issue for him. There are nods of approval when he says this.

So what do they think about Thornton Hall, the proposed new prison that would see them move from the city centre out to North County Dublin? One of the reasons Minister McDowell has used to argue in favour of the change is the fact that it would be easier to control the supply of drugs into the prison if it were further out of town. Given the importance of drugs to the men we have met, I expect them to rubbish this proposal as well.

But I am surprised. The men we talk to about this at least think that any new building would be an improvement on the current set-up. I ask about the extra distance, whether that would cause problems for families coming in on visits, but most still say that any new replacement for a building they heartily detest is a good thing. They're still slopping out, they can shower only once a week, it's unclean and unhygienic they say. They want a modern prison, with modern toilet facilities.

This leads on to the question about life behind bars, and whether it's the cushy number often criticised in public debate. I point out that many voters think prisoners should have a tougher and longer time behind bars than at present, on the basis that it might deter them from further crime. Once again everyone is talking, about the slopping out, the food, being locked up in your cell from seven o'clock at night, being away from your family. Andy says even if it is their fault that they're in Mountjoy in the first place, doing the time is far from easy. The worst parts are missing your family and the boredom. Andy is facing a long sentence for armed robbery and he doesn't think anyone outside would care, they prefer to think he's having an easy time of it, but he's not. He talks about the boredom again, and how he'd got himself off drugs outside, but he's back on them now.

By now it's coming up to lunchtime, and the men start to lose interest in us and drift away to queue up for their lunches, which are served in Styrofoam takeaway boxes. The temporary novelty caused by our visit has worn off; food and routine take over. But our guide won't let us leave until we have descended more stairs and clanged through more locked doors to Mountjoy's prison museum.

It's a fascinating place. The cells still look the same, but then we're shown the heavy shackles and leg irons the prisoners of the nineteenth century used to wear, the stiff prison uniforms, the restraints and headmasks. There are the execution books, with forty-six entries. There is Kevin Barry's name, in neat handwriting, on the list of those executed within the walls. There is the table of calculations worked out by the hangman to give the correct length of rope and drop to hang the guilty, no matter how tall or small, heavy or slight. The nooses are still kept in tin boxes: a soft leather collar around the rope an odd act of consideration for those who were to be hanged. There was always a spare noose in case the hangman had made a mistake in his calculations and the rope broke. We are shown the cat o' nine tails – the knotted rope whip that was used for official floggings when they were an accepted punishment in Her Majesty's Model Prison. However awful Mountjoy is now for its inmates, it's hard to grasp just how awful these conditions must have been for those who had to endure them. There's a record of the death of a seven-year-old boy who fell ill while incarcerated behind these walls, the youngest person ever to die in this jail.

But as we climb back up those steps and walk through the gates, with the keys turning behind us, it occurs to me that the other huge difference between now and then is not just the standard of treatment of prisoners, it is drugs. In the nineteenth and early twentieth century drugs would not have dominated the lives of those who passed through Mountjoy in the same way. Even when they get out of Mountjoy, many of the men we have met this morning will never be free of their addiction. Most of them didn't seem to think that any general election could make a difference to that, nor to much else in their marginalised lives. Their preoccupation was survival in a world where a needle in the arm or a powder up your nose is the only escape you can rely on, inside or outside the walls of Mountjoy. Except that it's no escape. It's a trap.

Áine Lawlor joined RTÉ in September 1984. She currently co-presents 'Morning Ireland', the flagship morning news programme on RTÉ Radio 1. She joined the team in April

1996 and is now one of RTÉ's most seasoned broadcasters, as well as one of Ireland's most recognised voices.

XIII. The 29th Dáil

Brian Dowling

Bertie Ahern could be excused a few quiet moments of personal triumph as he surveys the changed political landscape since he first became Taoiseach in 1997. Such has been his political acumen and dominance that the two main opposition parties, Fine Gael and the Labour party, are each on their third leader to face him across the Dáil chamber. If Democratic Left is included, Ahern has seen off six party leaders since becoming Taoiseach: two from Fine Gael (John Bruton, Michael Noonan); two from Labour (Dick Spring, Ruairi Quinn); one Democratic Left (Proinsias De Rossa); and one Progressive Democrat (Mary Harney). Sinn Féin's Gerry Adams is the only other party leader to stay the course over the last decade. The outcome of Election 2007 will determine whether Ahern will join the ranks of former leaders, or whether he will emerge once again as Taoiseach and witness the almost inevitable leadership contests amongst the losers.

Election 2002 was a tour de force for Fianna Fáil, bringing the party within touching distance of its unspoken but still cherished Holy Grail: the overall majority. Only for the razor-like, mid-campaign intervention of Michael McDowell with his 'Single Party Government – No Thanks' slogan, Fianna Fáil was on course to crash through the magical eighty-three seats to secure government on its own terms. McDowell's *blitzkrieg* was enough to scare off sufficient voters worried about the prospect of Fianna Fáil alone in government. Nonetheless, the party was tantalisingly close to an overall majority, with eighty-one seats. Given those numbers, Bertie Ahern didn't actually need the PDs to form a government. He could have relied on the so-called Fianna Fáil gene pool – those independent TDs whose support, at a price, would have ensured a single-party administration.

Typically cautious, and with an eye to stormy waters ahead, Ahern opted to have the PDs, with eight seats, back at the Cabinet table. Safely in office, the two government partners got down to business while the main opposition parties picked up the pieces. Fine Gael could only survey the wreckage of a disastrous campaign. For its part, Labour was stagnant.

Overall, Fine Gael lost twenty-three seats, with nine of those going in Dublin and leaving the party with just three TDs in the capital. Former ministers like the late Jim Mitchell, Nora Owen and Alan Dukes were among the political casualties. In the immediate aftermath of the election Michael Noonan quit as leader of Fine Gael, to be replaced by Enda Kenny.

Within weeks Ruairí Quinn took his leave of the Labour leadership, with Pat Rabbitte emerging as a convincing winner on a platform to provide the electorate with a clear choice of an alternative government at the next election. For the two main opposition leaders it was a case of back to the drawing board as they set about re-organising their respective party machines.

The first test for the two new leaders came in the summer of 2004 with the local and European elections. Against all expectations, Fine Gael delivered an election result that put it almost neck and neck with Fianna Fáil nationally. Two years of hard work paid off for Kenny. Labour only managed to repeat its 2002 share of the vote.

Still, the genesis of an alternative coalition was beginning to take shape. Co-operation between the two was taken to a new level with the launch of the Mullingar Accord in September 2004. If the local and European elections brought revival and hope to Fine Gael, they unleashed a terrible backlash on the government, especially on Fianna Fáil.

The glow of the 2002 election victory began to fade later that year, and throughout 2003 several polls showed a sharp decline in support for Fianna Fáil. Fine Gael and Labour tapped into a well of public anger over the aftermath of the general election. The 'feel-good' factor and the promises that the good times would keep rolling had evaporated quickly. The boom in public spending in the year leading up to the 2002 contest had to be reined in swiftly once the election was out of the way. When these corrective measures dovetailed with an economic downturn, the Fianna Fáil/PD coalition was on the backfoot.

It provided the opposition with the chance to exploit the public sentiment that Fianna Fáil and the PDs had 'conned' the electorate in 2002. Fianna Fáil saw its poll support slump into the low thirties. One man took the brunt of the growing hostility. As Minister for Finance, Charlie McCreevy had masterminded the tax-cutting strategy of the first administration and taken much of the credit for election planning and success in 2002. Now he was being blamed by the public and by Fianna Fáil back-benchers for the ills besetting the government. The more the criticisms mounted, the more McCreevy dug in, and the more the opposition singled him out as depicting the arrogance of a government that was too long in power.

Fianna Fáil strategists were expecting to lose support in the June 2004 local and European elections. But they, and the party leadership, were shocked by the scale of the collapse in their vote. After the votes were counted in the local elections, the party had managed to win only a 30 per cent share of the national vote. It was a long, steep fall from the 42 per cent secured in the general election.

If repeated in the next general election, the party faced a meltdown on a par with that suffered by Fine Gael in 2002. The inevitable soul-searching commenced. Rumblings began in Fianna Fáil that the party's electoral future would be salvaged only if McCreevy became EU Commissioner. In the months prior to the local and European elections a perception had taken root that the European Commissioner position was there for the taking, if Charlie McCreevy wanted it.

The only problem was that McCreevy showed all the signs of a man who wanted to complete a second term as Minister for Finance. Speaking in Cork, in the wake of the local and European elections, the Minister made clear his wish to remain in that post, adding that he had no travel plans either 'internally or externally'. That remark was seen as a signal that he was not for moving in the looming Cabinet reshuffle nor, for that matter, out of Cabinet to Brussels.

Within a month he was the Taoiseach's nominee as Ireland's new Commissioner. No matter how hard the Taoiseach and his Minister for Finance insisted that they had agreed this move as far back as the previous September, it was greeted with scepticism.

The most outspoken and controversial member of the Cabinet was on his way out, and Fianna Fáil moved with alacrity to embrace a 'softer, gentler' image at the party's September 'think-in' at Inchydoney, County Cork. Any doubts about the repositioning of the party were dispelled when it was announced that the keynote speaker would be Fr Sean Healy of CORI (Conference of Religious of Ireland).

Fr Healy is a committed anti-poverty campaigner and a stern critic of the McCreevy economic philosophy. For his part, McCreevy was dismissive of Fr Healy, regarding his prescription as a recipe for economic disaster.

Addressing the assembled Fianna Fáil Ministers, TDs and Senators, Fr Healy urged a dramatic change of direction in budgetary policy. He had a willing and receptive audience. There was no escaping the symbolism. Fianna Fáil was not just distancing itself from the McCreevy era, it wanted to be seen to be making the break. The Minister for Finance departed in late September, triggering the much-awaited Cabinet reshuffle.

The changes reflected the mood at Inchydoney, with Brian Cowen replacing McCreevy at the helm in the Department of Finance. His mandate was simple: for the remainder of the government's term budgetary generosity would be directed towards the low-paid and the under-privileged.

That change was well flagged, but the reshuffle also produced one of the biggest political gambles in recent history. Much to the astonishment of friends and foes alike, Mary Harney volunteered to become Minister for Health & Children. It was a courageous decision, and one that may yet have a profound influence on the political fate of Fianna Fáil and the PDs.

A re-shaped Government began planning for the December Budget that would deliver on the CORI agenda. Three weeks out from the Budget, the Taoiseach embodied the transformation by declaring he was 'one of the few socialists left in Irish politics'.

By the year end another major political figure was also moving on. Former Taoiseach and Fine Gael leader John Bruton was appointed the first EU Ambassador to the United States of

America, a decision reflecting his extensive political experience and a lifelong commitment to European ideals.

The departure of McCreevy and Bruton paved the way for two by-elections in Kildare and Meath in March 2005, which provided another test for government and opposition alike. Fine Gael's Shane McEntee held the party seat in Meath, while Independent candidate Catherine Murphy made the breakthrough in Kildare.

When Election 2007 gets underway the contestants will fight on terrain decided by five people not affiliated to any party. High Court judge Mr Justice Vivian Lavin, Kieran Coughlan (Clerk of the Dáil), Deirdre Lane (Clerk of the Seanad), Niall Callan (Secretary General of the Department of the Environment, Heritage and Local Government) and Emily O'Reilly (Ombudsman) comprised the Constituency Commission. That statutory body is charged with the delicate and, more often than not, controversial task of deciding the constituency boundaries.

For some politicians their decisions, based on detailed analysis of population trends, can prove crucial to their political survival. Throughout most of 2003 TDs eagerly awaited news from the Commission on the battlelines for the next general election. The waiting ended in January 2004 when details emerged of sweeping changes ahead. Fianna Fáil's Cork South Central deputy, Batt O'Keeffe, had just walked into the main hall of Leinster House when a colleague beckoned him. His colleague had just got a copy of the report of the Constituency Commission and they huddled in a corner, poring over its recommendations.

It recommended changes on a scale greater than expected. Almost two-thirds of the Dáil constituencies were to be revised, with a recommendation for an overall increase in the number of constituencies from forty-two to forty-three. When O'Keeffe looked at the details of the proposals for his political base he was stunned: 'I couldn't believe what I was reading, I felt there had to be a mistake. This simply couldn't be correct. I was shocked.'

O'Keeffe had helped Fianna Fáil win three out of five seats in Cork South Central in 2002. The Constituency Commission had redrawn the boundary line and his political base in Ballincollig, with a population of over 15,000, was to move to Cork North East. That change, O'Keeffe reckoned, would cost him about 60 per cent of his first-preference votes if he remained in Cork South Central.

His dilemma was typical of the kind of unforeseen changes that can be thrown up by the Commission. Nor was he alone in facing potential electoral pitfalls.

Taking account of increases and shifts in population, the Commission proposed a reduction in the number of five-seat constituencies from fourteen to twelve; an increase from twelve to thirteen in the number of four-seat constituencies and an increase from sixteen to eighteen in the number of three-seat constituencies.

The forty-third constituency arose from the decision to allocate an extra seat to Meath and divide it into two three-seat constituencies. Other key changes included: an extra Dáil seat for Kildare North and Dublin Mid-West; a reduction of one Dáil seat in Cork North Central and Dublin North Central; and one less seat for the combined counties of Sligo, Leitrim, Roscommon and Longford, with the establishment of three new constituencies named Sligo–North Leitrim (three seats), Roscommon–South Leitrim (three seats) and Longford–Westmeath (four seats).

Smaller parties and independents worried that the increase in smaller constituencies would prove more favourable to the bigger parties. Yet the situation facing Batt O'Keeffe shows that this is far from universally true. He opted to move and run in Cork North East, pitting his own survival alongside or, more likely, against that of his two party colleagues.

In Dublin North Central the Independent Finian McGrath will be under severe pressure to hold on in a three-seat constituency containing Sean Haughey, Ivor Callely and Richard Bruton. If McGrath faces difficulties in holding his seat, the former Labour TD and now Senator, Derek McDowell, has an even higher hill to climb to win back his Dáil seat in that constituency.

Three years on from the Constituency Commission report the politicians, who accept the independence of the Commission, have come to terms with the changes, even if some remain fearful about the likely impact.

It didn't take long before Mary Harney discovered what many before her had found. The Department of Health & Children is a political minefield, or 'Angola' as it was dubbed by Brian Cowen. Despite those difficulties, her position as Tánaiste and leader of the PDs never seemed in doubt. At least, that was how it appeared. Behind the scenes a struggle was ensuing between Harney and Michael McDowell, the Minister for Justice, who believed he had an understanding that she would relinquish the leadership as early as December 2005.

The tensions within the party erupted publicly in June 2006 as the details of the leadership row spilled beyond the previously sealed party doors. A letter from the party's trustees, detailed in *The Irish Times*, spoke of a dysfunctional relationship between Harney and McDowell. For a period the party looked on the verge of imploding into two factions, until an uneasy peace was declared with an agreement that Harney would remain as leader until after the general election.

Over the summer months Harney relented, and in September announced her resignation as party leader. McDowell, as widely expected, emerged as leader without a contest. He had barely assumed the mantle of leader and Tánaiste when controversy erupted over payments to the Taoiseach in the early 1990s. Ahern faced intense pressure to explain the payments and opted for a personalised, heartfelt appeal to the nation in an extended interview on RTÉ's '6.1 News'. Stressing the personal circumstances of his marriage break-up, Ahern said a number of friends gave him IR£39,000 in loans in 1993. He also referred to another payment given by businessmen during a trip he made to Manchester in 1994.

Some of the accounts provided by the Taoiseach were difficult to decipher, and he was unable to provide a list of the businessmen in Manchester who gave him stg£8,000. Pressure intensified when it emerged that one of the businessmen present in Manchester had been the previous owner of the Taoiseach's house. When McDowell and the PDs went silent for twenty-four hours, the fate of the coalition appeared to hang in the balance. Fianna Fáil let it be known that the PDs could leave government if they wished, but that Fianna Fáil would remain in office. The party had maintained strong lines of contact with the 'gene-pool' and sufficient support was available to sustain them in government.

The stand-off was resolved with a face-saving formula of new changes in ethics legislation. As the Taoiseach and Tánaiste announced it was back to business as usual, McDowell, believing recording had finished, remarked: 'We survived it.'

Polls in the wake of the controversy showed an extraordinary recovery by the main government party. The findings confounded politicians across party lines – not least the opposition parties, which were suffering most from the fallout over the payments to the Taoiseach. It demonstrated, yet again, the extent to which Ahern is the commanding figure in Irish politics.

By late January this year a new poll suggested the contest between the coalition and the Fine Gael/Labour alternative was still open. It was 'game on' once more. The volatility in the polls, the issues, the changes in constituencies and those events no one can predict will all help shape the campaign battles that lie ahead in Election 2007. So, too, will the number of sitting TDs who are retiring.

At the time of writing, no fewer than twenty TDs have declared they will not contest the election. Half of those are Fianna Fáil deputies: Joe Jacob, Joe Walsh, Dermot Fitzpatrick, Tony Dempsey, Síle de Valera, Dan Wallace, Eoin Ryan, GV Wright, Jim Glennon and Liam Aylward. Michael Collins, who is also retiring, commenced the 29th Dáil as a member of the Fianna Fáil parliamentary party, but resigned the whip after his name appeared on a list of tax defaulters.

Fine Gael is losing Paul McGrath, Dinny McGinley and Gay Mitchell. Three Labour TDs are stepping down: Joe Sherlock, Sean Ryan and Seamus Pattison. Two Independents, Mildred Fox and Marian Harkin, have also declared that they will not contest the election. The destination of these twenty seats will also prove crucial to the formation of the next government.

Brian Dowling joined the political staff of RTÉ in January 2007. He was appointed Political Correspondent of the *Irish Independent* in 1993 and has been a political journalist since then. He was Irish Political Editor of the *Sunday Times* between 2001 and 2003, and then returned to the *Irish Independent*. Throughout that period he was a regular contributor to RTÉ's current affairs programmes and will be involved in RTÉ's coverage of Election 2007.

The Constituencies

Rachael English & Nick Coffey

Introduction

Rachael English

Albert Reynolds introduced a number of phrases to the Irish political lexicon. As is often the way, the ones most frequently quoted are probably those of which he is least proud. 'Total crap', 'That's women for you'. It is unlikely that the former Taoiseach was the first to claim that every General Election is actually forty-something separate elections. But it is a phrase that's widely attributed to him. And as a political maxim, it has never been more popular. But is it true? Well, having visited most of the country's constituencies over the past few months, I'm afraid the answer is it is, and it isn't!

In two very different ways, the 1992 and 2002 general elections showed that it can be very hard to buck a national trend. Your reputation for being a great man to get the street lights fixed can count for very little if your party is in meltdown. Conversely, even your neighbours might have trouble recognising you, but if your party is flying high you could find yourself in Leinster House.

The Labour surge of 1992 led to gains that even the most astute local observer could not have foreseen. How many pundits predicted that Dr Moosajee Bhamjee would take a seat in Clare or that Eithne Fitzgerald would go from also-ran to almost two quotas in Dublin South?

It's true that there was a general belief before the last election in 2002 that Fine Gael was in big trouble. But very few observers guessed that polling day would prove to be quite so catastrophic. One political correspondent told me recently that, on the night before the election, he drew up a list of how many seats he thought each party would win. He couldn't get Fine Gael beyond the high thirties and reckoned that he must be overstating the party difficulties; Fine Gael won thity-one seats.

All of this doesn't mean that local factors are unimportant. They can play a huge role. Many people vote on local issues and they vote for local candidates. An unknown can win a Dáil seat, but he or she won't hold on to it unless they're seen to 'do the work'.

That's why Willie Penrose of Labour topped the poll in Westmeath last time out, long after other beneficiaries of the 'Spring Tide' had been given more time to spend with their families. It's why Independent candidate James Breen topped the poll in Clare even though most national pundits had never heard of him. It's why, no matter what emanates from Dublin Castle, Michael Lowry continues to get an enormous vote in Tipperary North.

There was an understandable furore recently over Junior Minister Tony Killeen's representations on behalf of a convicted murderer. The wonder is that such a controversy hadn't arisen before. The majority of TDs still send out huge volumes of correspondence even though they know it may have little effect. They still fill in forms, lobby Ministers and make representations to County Councils even if all they achieve for a constituent is something to which that person was entitled anyway.

I've been in constituency offices where the teetering piles of paperwork are displayed as a badge of political honour. And the fact is that some representatives do this even when they believe it's a waste of time and their energies would be better spent elsewhere.

You're unlikely, however, to find many prominent political figures who will publicly admit this. One TD, who is well known for his assiduous constituency work, told me – off the record – that he thought this way of doing things was outmoded and pointless.

When I asked why he continued to operate this system with such vigour, he answered that if he didn't, his opponents would.

So for all of the changes in Ireland over the past decade, the old clientellist system lives on. This is not entirely negative. A string of surveys have shown that Irish people are far more likely to have met one of their local representatives than voters in many other European countries. That's surely a good thing.

But sometimes the system becomes a parody of itself. Having an informal chat in one constituency, I asked why there was a view that a particular TD could be in trouble.

'His heart's not in it', was the reply, 'I gather there are local funerals where he hasn't been seen.'

There are a couple of factors which may lead to the erosion of this type of politics. Several TDs pointed out to me that younger people are, in general, more aware of their entitlements than their parents' generation. They are more likely to look up a relevant website than to dial the local constituency office. A number of regional journalists told me that, in their area, more of the old-style constituency work was being hoovered up by ambitious county councillors. The increase in pay and the abolition of the dual mandate have certainly led to a rise in the number of full-time councillors.

In this regard, it's worth pointing out that the majority of Dáil hopefuls who I have met over recent months are working full-time on their campaign. I remember one candidate telling me plaintively that he was likely to be the only person on the ballot paper who had a proper non-political job.

Never underestimate either the simple power of living in the right place. Irish people continue to vote local. It's why the two big parties, in particular, obsess about getting the right geographical spread of candidates.

There can be no better example than this: in the Louth constituency in 2002 when a Fianna Fáil candidate called Frank Maher was eliminated, more of his second preferences went to the Fine Gael candidate, Fergus O'Dowd, than to his own party colleague, Seamus Kirk. Both Maher and O'Dowd are from Drogheda. Kirk is from the north of the county. Louth may be the smallest county in Ireland, but its geographical divide is of epic proportions.

This helps to explain why two particular political obsessions continue to thrive. The first of these is the need for every town to 'have a voice'. 'A Strong Voice for (fill in name of town/county/electoral area as appropriate)' must be the most overused line in Irish electioneering. This inevitably leads to the second fixation – the perceived importance of having a local man or woman at the cabinet table. A constituency without a State car is not a happy place. A constituency without so much as a Junior Minister, Carlow/Kilkenny for example, is a very miserable place indeed.

In all of this you'll have noticed that one element is missing: policy. It's a gross over-simplification to say that policies don't matter. Of course, they do. But it also must be acknowledged that, in 2002, the issues and the policy differences often ended up at the margins of the media coverage.

A fascinating piece of work called the Irish Election Study, which will be published in full later in the year, suggests that issues weren't at the forefront of many voters' minds either. Researchers from the Economic and Social Research Institute asked more than two and a half thousand people about the reasons why they voted the way they did. This was more than a snapshot. The questionnaire took over an hour to complete. Academics from Trinity and UCD have been poring over the data ever since.

Put at their most simple the findings suggest that, as far as the voters of 2002 were concerned, a general sense of economic competence won the day for the outgoing government. The nitty-gritty of individual policy pledges was far less influential than whether a voter had met the candidate. There's a reason why Irish politicians are so obsessed with the pre-election canvass. It works.

There is little doubt that the health service remains the number one issue as far as many people are concerned. It gets top billing in almost every opinion poll. It lights up the phones on radio programmes like 'Liveline'. In my journey around the constituencies it has been mentioned more than any other topic.

Yet, in 2002, in several of those places where it was a live issue, people tended to eschew the opposition for a local single-issue candidate. From Cavan/Monaghan (Paudge Connolly) to Wexford (Liam Twomey, who has since joined Fine Gael) to Mayo (Jerry Cowley) to Dublin North Central (Finian McGrath) it appeared that while many voters were angry with the government they didn't have that much faith in the main opposition parties either.

It can still be foolish to make easy assumptions. I remember meeting one woman in Cork who was absolutely spitting about problems with the health service,

'So', I asked her, 'Is your vote there for the taking then?'

'Oh, not at all', was the reply, 'I'm a member of Fianna Fáil'.

* * *

For an illustration of how many things in Ireland have changed and how many remain the same go to a place like Roscommon Town in the newly-formed Roscommon/South Leitrim constituency. Massive 24-hour supermarket? Check. Eastern European food shop? Check. Raging controversy about the future of the local hospital? Check.

Also regularly mentioned in my travels has been the sort of

issues that first came to the fore during the 2005 by-elections in Meath and Kildare North. Catherine Murphy, another Independent and the victor in the latter constituency, argues that the national political agenda was reshaped by those campaigns. Aspiring TDs were met with a barrage of complaints about the lack of school places, the paucity of affordable childcare, about traffic gridlock and overcrowded trains.

These have been referred to as 'quality of life' issues, but that is a very wishy-washy label for matters that can really enrage people. There are now many men and women of working age who don't remember the years of recession and emigration. Telling them they're lucky to have a job doesn't really cut it.

It's also true that sometimes journalists focus on personal rivalries rather than on complex policy issues because that's the easier thing to do. And, let's be honest, feuds and fallings-out are very entertaining. Multi-seat constituencies tend to throw up amazing rivalries. And, in quite a few places, there's no rivalry as keen as that between two party colleagues. The old adage about the importance of keeping your enemies close but your friends closer is still being played out in many of the forty-three constituencies.

I have been told wonderfully scurrilous stories about members of all parties. Even though the odd one might actually be true, very few are fit for broadcast.

So what's going to happen on Election Day? Who's going to be the next Taoiseach and who will be joining him at the cabinet table? The simple fact is that none of us know. Even though, as I've learnt, the country is filled with people who think that they do.

Whether you go through the battles constituency by constituency, or whether you extrapolate figures from the national opinion polls, the chances are that in some cases you'll be right and in many you'll be wrong.

It has been a necessary part of 'The Constituency' that, having spoken about the candidates and the issues, local political watchers are asked about the most likely outcome on polling day. But no matter how experienced, diligent and skilful they are it's still just guesswork. It really is like tipping horses only, in some cases, with rather more intellectual snobbery.

It should also be said that sometimes those of us engaged in this guesswork tend to forget about a little matter called voting. It's up to the entire country to decide the 166 names that will make up the next Dáil. And, as voters, many of our decisions will be predictable and a few will cause a stir.

Some people place a number beside a name because they have a clear preference for the make-up of the next Government. Some people put the same number beside the same name because the candidate helped them with a planning application. Some people just can't think of anybody else to vote for.

When the votes are counted, there will be equivalents of Paul Gogarty of the Green Party in Dublin Mid West or Independent Paddy McHugh in Galway East; perceived outsiders will be elected. There will also be equivalents of Fianna Fáil's Mary O'Rourke in Westmeath and fine Gael's PJ Sheehan in Cork South West; perceived certainties will lose their seats.

Experience shows that it is nigh on impossible to say exactly what's going to happen several months out from an election. The national trends are still a bit murky. New candidates emerge. Old candidates withdraw. Fresh issues appear. Momentum gathers.

It would also seem that the further away from polling day you are, the greater the tendency to be cautious in your predictions. A few of the predictions in this book are rather less conservative than those voiced on the radio programme. But they could still be too conservative.

For instance, I've spoken to a number of independent observers who feel that the Green Party may gain seats, but they aren't quite sure where those gains are going to be. There could also be more seat-swapping within parties. Five years ago, how many pundits were sure that Mary O'Rourke would be ousted by Donie Cassidy?

There is one other phenomenon that deserves a mention. I've been to constituencies where a candidate or a party worker or a journalist has pointed out a new housing estate and said,

'But we haven't a clue how most of those people are going to vote.'

According to the census figures, forty out of the forty-three constituencies have seen a rise in population since 2002. The huge increases in areas like Dublin North and Dublin West have been well-documented. But there are also many places where the population growth has been slightly less marked, but could still be significant. For instance, in Cork East the number of people has risen by 15 per cent, in Laois/Offaly the increase is 12 per cent; it's 13 per cent in Wicklow and 9 per cent in Carlow/Kilkenny.

Quite a few of these new residents may not be eligible to vote. Some may not be registered. Some more may have no interest. But that still leaves plenty of new voters, many of them people who have moved into the constituency from another part of the country. These are voters who are less likely to be familiar with local candidates and political dynasties. They could have a completely different view of what matters and what doesn't.

The voter can be a pretty complex individual. Wouldn't it be an almighty shame if any of us could predict with absolute certainty what the country will decide?

Map of National Constituencies

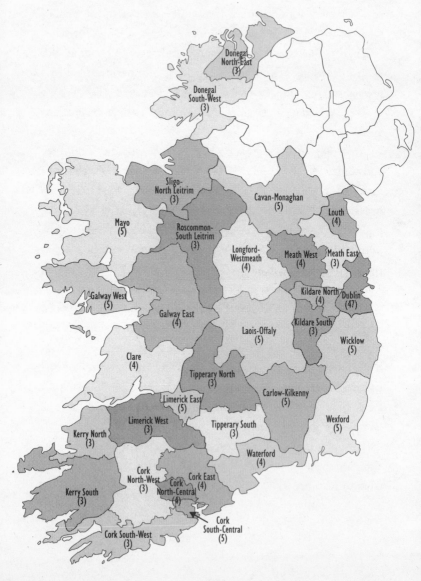

152

Map of Dublin Constituencies

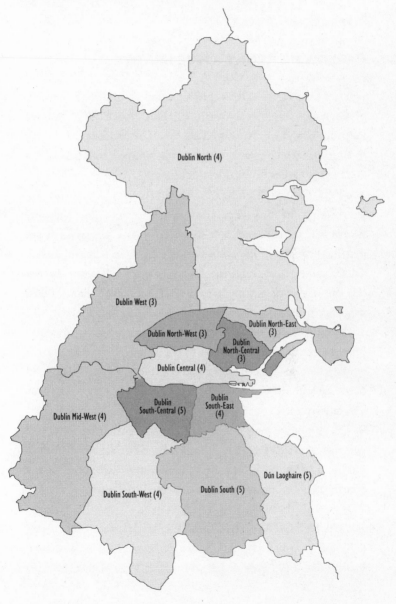

Dublin North (4)

Dublin West (3)

Dublin North-West (3)

Dublin North-East (3)

Dublin North-Central (3)

Dublin Central (4)

Dublin Mid-West (4)

Dublin South-Central (5)

Dublin South-East (4)

Dublin South-West (4)

Dublin South (5)

Dún Laoghaire (5)

XIV. The Constituencies, A-Z

Rachael English & Nick Coffey

CARLOW/KILKENNY – FIVE SEATS

THE SITTING DEPUTIES: Liam Aylward (FF), John McGuinness (FF), MJ Nolan (FF), Phil Hogan (FG), Seamus Pattison (Lab). Liam Aylward is also an MEP and is opting to stay in Brussels. Seamus Pattison, who was returned automatically in 2002 as the Ceann Comhairle, is retiring.

THE CONSTITUENCY: There is no more divided constituency that this. The Carlow vote stays in Carlow; Kilkenny people vote for Kilkenny candidates. Traditionally, this has meant that the majority of the constituency's TDs are Kilkenny-based. This became an election issue five years ago when it was claimed that the smaller county might have no TD. In the event MJ Nolan was elected and Carlow maintained its Dáil representation.

Parts of Carlow have become 'commuter country' in recent years with considerable numbers of people travelling to Dublin for work. There have been some high profile job losses locally, in particular with the closure of the sugar factory. Kilkenny maintains a significant rural vote.

The number of people living in Carlow/Kilkenny has risen by 9 per cent since 2002, with the rate of growth slightly higher in Carlow. Despite this Kilkenny still has almost two thirds of the constituency's population and will elect at least three of the five TDs.

THE LEADING CANDIDATES: McGuinness (FF), Nolan (FF) and Hogan (FG), plus Bobby Aylward (FF), Senator John Paul Phelan (FG), Senator Fergal Browne (FG), Michael O'Brien

(Lab), Jim Townsend (Lab), Walter Lacey (PD), Kathleen Funchion (SF)

THE CAMPAIGN: Carlow/Kilkenny was one of Fianna Fáil's big successes in 2002. Because of Seamus Pattison's automatic return only four seats were up for decision. Fianna Fáil took three of them with 50 per cent of the vote. The losers were Fine Gael. John Browne retired and his son Fergal failed to win the seat. Browne the younger's elimination secured Phil Hogan's election.

On this occasion, there is a widespread view that three of the candidates are all but assured of election. The first of these is John McGuinness of Fianna Fáil. In 2002, Liam Aylward topped the poll with more than a quota; his brother Bobby is expected to replace him in the Dáil, but his vote is unlikely to be quite so high. Fine Gael's Phil Hogan is also in a strong position. All three are from Kilkenny.

This leaves a considerable number of candidates in contention for the remaining two seats. Likely to be among them are Mary White, MJ Nolan, John Paul Phelan, Fergal Browne, Michael O'Brien and Jim Townsend. Various party people and journalists will put forward various reasons as to why any of these six could take a seat.

There will be considerable pressure on Phil Hogan, who is Fine Gael's director of organisation, to deliver a second seat here. John Paul Phelan is a serious contender, but he is based in south Kilkenny. Fergal Browne, on the other hand, is the only Fine Gael candidate in Carlow and has a geographical advantage. If Browne were to be successful, MJ Nolan might lose out as he did in 1997. On the other hand, Nolan should be helped by transfers from the PD candidate, Councillor Walter Lacey ,who is also from Carlow.

Could Labour be vulnerable? It had been widely anticipated that the Pattison name would live on in Carlow/Kilkenny politics through Seamus Pattison's nephew Eoin, but he lost out the party convention and the ticket consists of two veterans, Michael O'Brien in Kilkenny and Jim Townsend in Carlow. There is a very strong Labour tradition in this constituency – Seamus Pattison has been *in situ* for more than forty years.

Carlow/Kilkenny is high up on the Green Party's list of targets, as it was in 2002. The party's deputy leader, Mary White, is a county councillor for the Borris electoral area in Carlow. In the last general election she got just over 8 per cent of the vote. It had been speculated that this time the Greens would run a second candidate, Kilkenny-based councillor, Malcolm Noonan. This has been ruled out by the party who argue that Mary White's support is well spread across the two counties. In general, national pundits have tended to rate her chances more highly than local journalists. A factor White may have in her favour is that Sinn Féin transferred quite strongly to the Greens in 2002 and she can probably expect a similar boost on this occasion.

OUR PREDICTION: McGuinness, Aylward and Hogan should be elected. Other than that it's wide open.

If Fine Gael are to gain a seat their vote will have to be close to the 29 per cent they achieved here in 1997. Quite a lot could depend, too, on the order in which candidates are eliminated. With no great confidence, we're opting for a second seat for Fine Gael, for Fianna Fail's MJ Nolan to lose out, for Labour to take a seat and for Mary White of the Greens to fall just short. Having said that, the Greens are likely to make gains in this election and, if they get a reasonable bounce, Mary White has a big chance. Nevertheless, we'll go for an overall outcome of 2 FF 2FG 1 Lab – a gain for FG from FF.

CAVAN/MONAGHAN – FIVE SEATS

OUTGOING DEPUTIES: Rory O'Hanlon (FF), Brendan Smith (FF), Seymour Crawford (FG), Caoimhín Ó Caolain (SF), Paudge Connolly (Ind).

THE CONSTITUENCY: Cavan/Monaghan stretches almost the breadth of the country, from Inniskeen in County Monaghan, on the Louth border, right over to Blacklion in County Cavan, on the Leitrim border.

It's the constituency of Rory O'Hanlon, who as Ceann Comhairle, is returned automatically. This effectively reduces Cavan/Monaghan to four seats.

THE LEADING CANDIDATES: All the outgoing deputies plus Joe O'Reilly (FG). Fianna Fáilhave yet to select a Monaghan-based candidate to join Brendan Smith.

THE CAMPAIGN: The principal question thrown up in Cavan/Monaghan is whether Paudge Connolly, the surprise winner in 2002, can hold onto his seat. He ran as an Independent, on the issue of retaining the services at Monaghan General Hospital. He took votes from both Fianna Fáil and Fine Gael. The Fianna Fáil vote was down by 3.5 per cent, Fine Gael's by 9 per cent. Those figures would suggest that Fine Gael paid the electoral price for Fianna Fáil policies. As the constituency will only elect four deputies this time Connolly has got his back to the wall.

Fianna Fáil's failure to so far finalise their election team has left that party, in Monaghan in particular, in some disarray. The Sinn Féin seat is seen as being so secure, that there's little or no speculation about Caoimhín Ó Caolain's expected performance.

Fine Gael were the losers here in 2002, and you can expect their Cavan-based candidate, Joe O'Reilly, to make great play of the fact that Cavan, with a greater population than Monaghan, currently only one of the five deputies here, Brendan Smith.

OUR PREDICTION: Fianna Fáil, Fine Gael and Sinn Féin will all win seats. That will leave Connolly battling for survival. Most people see the greatest threat to the Connolly seat coming from Fianna Fáil. But county loyalties could just work to O'Reilly's advantage. He could be the surprise packet this time.

There have been rumours that Fianna Fáil have approached Connolly to join their ticket. He is adamant that he run as an independent. If that's the case, the increased quota might prove to be too much for him. Fianna Fáil have to be favourites to take the independent seat. With Rory O'Hanlon automatically returned, that could leave them with three of the five seats.

3 FF, 1 FG, 1 SF. (FF gain from IND)

CLARE – FOUR SEATS

OUTGOING DEPUTIES: Tony Killeen (FF), Síle de Valera (FF), James Breen (Ind), Pat Breen (FG), Síle de Valera is retiring.

THE CONSTITUENCY: In 2002, a previously loyal (and low-profile) Fianna Fáil county councillor fell out with his party over their failure to select him as a general election candidate. He decided to run anyway, but was given little chance by the vast majority of observers. James Breen went on to top the poll with almost 20 per cent of the first preference vote, taking the seat of his former party colleague, Brendan Daly. He also proved how unpredictable this four-seat constituency can be. A decade previously, the big shock had been provided by the election of Dr Moosajee Bhamjee of the Labour Party.

In the county, James Breen is widely seen as having taken the highly volatile 'Feck the lot of you' vote.

Clare has seen a steady rise in population over the past fifteen years, with the bulk of the growth in and around the two largest towns, Ennis and Shannon. There has never been a TD from Shannon Town and its residents can expect a thorough canvassing from all of the parties. There have also been rumblings from west Clare where there is some unhappiness at the fact that there is currently no TD based in that part of the county.

The perennial issue in Clare is the future of Ennis General Hospital. It has been the subject of political controversy since its downgrading in the late 1980s. The future of Shannon Airport has been another constant over the past two decades, but the county has gradually become less reliant on the airport for jobs and it doesn't appear to be the issue it once was. Also, while the American military's use of the airport may raise hackles in many other parts of the country, it's unlikely to be a strong feature of the election campaign in Clare.

Neither should another of the big controversies of 2002 – the building of a road to bypass Ennis – be the centre of attention on this occasion. With perfect timing, the first phase of the long-promised bypass was opened in early 2007.

Under the latest boundary revision, Clare is losing a small amount of territory in the south east of the county to the Limerick East constituency.

THE LEADING CANDIDATES: Three of the four sitting deputies plus Senator Brendan Daly (FF), Senator Timmy Dooley (FF), Tony Mulcahy (FG), Madeleine Taylor Quinn (FG), Joe Carey (FG), Pascal Fitzgerald (Lab), Brian Meaney (Green), Anna Prior (SF)

THE CAMPAIGN: One of the big talking points of recent months has been whether the controversial representations made by Tony Killeen on behalf of a convicted murderer will harm his vote. Soundings suggest that while there is much disapproval of what he did, this is unlikely to have huge electoral consequences. The standing of the Minister of State, who is based in Kilnaboy in the north of the county, may have been damaged but he will still be elected. With Síle de Valera retiring, the other names on the ticket are the veteran Brendan Daly from Cooraclare in the west and the newcomer Tommy Dooley from Mountshannon in the east. Rumours that a fourth candidate would be added have come to nothing.

Of course, Tony Killeen isn't the only local deputy to have landed in trouble over a prisoner. Pat Breen had earlier been at the centre of a controversy over enquiries he had made about a convicted paedophile. This episode led to a further ratcheting up of the tensions in an already uneasy Fine Gael ticket. Fine Gael have decided to run four candidates in a four seat constituency where they only have one outgoing TD. County councillor Tony Mulcahy was chosen along with Breen at a selection convention. The names of former TD, Madeleine Taylor Quinn and Councillor Joe Carey (son of another former TD, Donal Carey) were later added by party headquarters. Fine Gael claims it can win two seats, but it is fair to say that many people in the county, including its own supporters, are mystified by this strategy.

James Breen will be running again. His vote is likely to be down, but he can afford to shed quite a few votes and still return to Leinster House.

A reasonably strong performance will be expected from Brian Meaney of the Green Party in his third general election. Indeed, if there is a substantial swing to the Green across the country this is one place where they should be in with a shout. At the moment, however, it's hard to see the Ennis-based county councillor taking a seat.

As is the case in a considerable number of constituencies, there is also likely to be at least one more Independent candidate here, although none had been confirmed at the time of going to press. At this stage it's hard to see any such candidate having the same impact as James Breen in 2002.

OUR PREDICTION: For all of his travails, the safest seat is probably still that of Tony Killeen. There's also a belief that James Breen will be returned. An MRBI poll for TG4 suggested that Brendan Daly would take a second seat for Fianna Fáil. But the word is that Timmy Dooley has been doing a massive amount of canvassing and he could well overtake his Seanad colleague. Amid the Fine Gael collapse in 2002, the party still got 25 per cent of the Clare vote. There's certainly a seat here and outgoing TD , Pat Breen, is seen as the best-placed candidate. That would mean no change in Clare – 2 FF, 1 FG, 1 Ind.

Now, that all makes perfect sense but, as we've seen, Clare voters have an unpredictable streak. The wildcard this time could well be Tony Mulcahy, the man who shocked many in his own party when he was chosen at the Fine Gael selection convention. He is also the only candidate from Shannon Town – and Clare's population is increasingly based in the south of the county. He may not be there at the end, and the chances of Fine Gael taking a second seat are very small. But don't rule out a few more twists and turns before the final result is announced.

CORK EAST – FOUR SEATS

OUTGOING DEPUTIES: Ned O'Keeffe (FF), Michael Ahern (FF), David Stanton (FG), Joe Sherlock (Lab). Joe Sherlock is retiring.

THE CONSTITUENCY: Cork East is one of a string of constituencies where a member of the Fine Gael front bench, in this case the then-chief whip Paul Bradford, was ousted in 2002 and will be attempting to return to the Dáil this time. It's also one of a small number of constituencies where the toughest battle could be between Fine Gael and, their potential government partners, the Labour Party.

This is a large constituency, running from Mitchelstown in the north, down to Mallow and Fermoy, and on to Youghal, Midleton and Cobh. It has also seen a significant increase in population since 2002. According to the preliminary census figures, the constituency now has a population of just over 104,000. That's a 15 per cent rise in five years.

Prior to the last election many of the bigger issues appeared to be in the south of the constituency. There was particular focus on the closure of Youghal Carpets. This time, however, there's likely to be equal focus on the north.

The BUPA jobs in Fermoy may have been saved, but the closure of the sugar factory and the fate of the site remains an issue in Mallow. Another industrial casualty was FCI in Fermoy and there have been hundreds of redundancies at Dairygold in Mitchelstown. A further issue mentioned frequently by people in the northern end of the constituency is the fate of Mallow Hospital, which locals claim is underfunded. In the south, particularly in the Cobh area, there is still considerable controversy about proposals for a toxic waste incinerator in Cork Harbour.

THE LEADING CANDIDATES: Three of the four outgoing deputies plus Paul Bradford (FG), Séan Sherlock (Lab), John Mulvihill (Lab), Sandra McLellan (SF), Sarah Iremonger (Green)

THE CAMPAIGN: Despite the jobs and health issues, there's a general consensus that Fianna Fáil's two TDs, Ned O'Keeffe from Mitchelstown and the Minister of State at the Department of Enterprise, Trade and Employment, Michael Ahern from

Carrigtwohill, will be returned.

Midleton-based David Stanton is expected to be re-elected for Fine Gael.

The Sinn Féin candidate, Sandra McLellan, is a member of Youghal Town Council. A number of local observers expect her to poll reasonably strongly. She's likely to improve on the 6 per cent the party got here in 2002, but a seat seems a step too far.

OUR PREDICTION: On 'The Constituency', Ralph Riegel from the *Irish Independent* and Mary Smithwick of the *Evening Echo* felt that the contest for the final seat would be fought out between Paul Bradford and Séan Sherlock, who are both from the Mallow area. This seems to be a popular view, with opinion divided as to which of them will make it in the end. Sherlock is a son of Joe, the outgoing TD, and is seen as a strong candidate, but Fine Gael locally are investing a lot in their man's return.

This could be very, very close, but we'll go for Sherlock.

That would mean 2 FF, 1FG, 1 Lab – no change.

CORK NORTH CENTRAL – FOUR SEATS

OUTGOING DEPUTIES: Noel O'Flynn (FF), Billy Kelleher (FF), Danny Wallace (FF), Bernard Allen (FG), Kathleen Lynch (Lab). Danny Wallace is retiring.

THE CONSTITUENCY: Cork North Central is now reduced to a four-seater. It loses part of the city centre – south of the North Channel of the Lee – and about 15,000 of its votes to Cork South Central. It gains about 4,000 votes from the Donoughmore and Inniscarra area, formerly in Cork North West. The constituency is now almost equally divided between rural and urban components.

THE LEADING CANDIDATES: All the outgoing deputies, except for Danny Wallace, who is retiring, plus Gerry Kelly (FG),

Jonathan O'Brien (SF), Chris O'Leary (GP), Mick Barry (SP), Ted tynan (WP)

THE CAMPAIGN: Sinn Féin are making noises that their man, Jonathan O'Brien, could be the dark horse here. It would be one of the biggest upsets of the election if there was to be any major change to the status quo. The decision by Danny Wallace to step down must considerably ease the concerns of the outgoing deputies seeking re-election, since Fianna Fáil are now running two candidates instead of three. Here, the Worker's Part have traditionally had a presence on the ballot paper and this time round Ted Tynan will be standing for the party.

OUR PREDICTION: Sinn Féin aspirations will be diluted by the Green and Socialist Party candidates. Its odds on that it will be a case of 'as you were' in Cork North Central.

2 FF. 1 FG. 1 Lab.

CORK NORTH WEST – THREE SEATS

OUTGOING DEPUTIES: Michael Moynihan (FF), Donal Moynihan (FF), Gerard Murphy (FG).

THE CONSTITUENCY: 'Fianna Fáil's Mayo' and 'The Constituency of Death' are the sort of labels being given to this sprawling three-seat constituency. It stretches from Charleville in the north though Kanturk and Macroom and almost as far south as Dunmanway.

A redrawing of the boundaries moved the town of Ballincollig and its hinterland from Cork South Central into Cork North West. Moving with it is the Minister of State at the Department of the Environment, Heritage and Local Government, Batt O'Keeffe. The problem for the party is that it already has two TDs here, the Macroom-based Donal Moynihan and Michael Moynihan who's from Kiskeam near Kanturk. The rivalry between them has become the stuff of local legend, with claims that when Bertie Ahern visited the constituency party workers had to put a stop-watch on him, so that the three got an equal amount of the leader's time!

THE LEADING CANDIDATES: The three sitting deputies plus Batt O'Keeffe (FF), Michael Creed (FG), Martin Coughlan (Lab). There is also likely to be Green Party candidate.

THE CAMPAIGN: Even the most optimistic Fianna Fáil supporter wouldn't argue that three out of three is possible. But there is a fighting chance of two seats. So which two would it be? Well, even though there aren't enough votes in Ballincollig alone to elect Batt O'Keeffe, he is the only candidate in that area and can expect a large chunk of what's available. He has also been working his new constituency for the past two years, and is widely tipped to take a seat. This, of course, means that one of the two (unrelated) Moynihans would have to lose out. Most local observers are very reluctant to pick between them. But there is a view that given the massive vote Michael Moynihan received in 2002 (he topped the poll with 1.09 of a quota) he would be the more likely survivor.

This brings us to Fine Gael, which in six successive elections took two out of three in Cork North West. Their vote management here was legendary. That pattern came to an abrupt end with the election of Michael Moynihan in 1997. The party is also likely to win one seat this year.

There was a big surprise here last time when, in his first general election, Gerard Murphy from Newmarket replaced his party colleague Michael Creed. Creed is steeped in Fine Gael. His father Donal was a TD, his grandfather was a county councillor, and he was widely seen as a certainty for re-election. In the end, it was incredibly close with Murphy winning the seat by fewer than 100 votes on the final count.

They will also be the party's two candidates this summer and, again, it could be difficult to separate them. Creed bounced back after defeat, taking a seat in the Macroom electoral area of Cork County Council in the 2004 local elections with almost 30 per cent of the vote, and local soundings suggest that he could prevail this time.

It should be said that Fine Gael don't see this as an either/or situation. Senior party figures claim that they will win two here.

Martin Coughlan, who's also a Macroom-based County Councillor, will be the Labour candidate. He ran here in 2002 and got just less than 7 per cent of the vote.

At the moment, it looks like the voters of Cork North West will have relatively few names to choose from. Whatever the changes elsewhere in the country, this is a constituency that remains dominated by Fianna Fáil and Fine Gael. Between them the big two took more than 90 per cent of the vote in the last General Election.

The relatively small number of candidates is unlikely to prevent people from going to the polling booth. In 2002 this constituency had the highest turnout in the country, with just over 73 per cent of those on the electoral register using their vote.

OUR PREDICTION: A Fine Gael gain can't be entirely dismissed. After all, even on its darkest day in 2002 the party got 42 per cent of the Cork North West vote. On balance, we'll go for two Fianna Fáil, one Fine Gael (no overall change in party numbers, but an expected change in personnel).

CORK SOUTH CENTRAL — FIVE SEATS

OUTGOING DEPUTIES: Michéal Martin (FF), Batt O'Keefe (FF), John Dennehy (FF), Simon Coveney (FG), Dan Boyle (GP).

THE CONSTITUENCY: Cork South Central sees significant boundary and population changes for this election. The North Channel of the River Lee will now be the dividing line between the two Cork City constituencies, South Central and North Central. The whole of the city centre is now in South Central giving it twenty-five thousand new voters. It loses about fifteen thousand votes from the Ballincollig area, which now moves to Cork North West. Some outlying pockets near Kinsale, with about four thousand votes moves into Cork South West.

THE LEADING CANDIDATES: For this election Batt O'Keefe (FF) moves with his Ballincollig base to Cork North West leaving the other four outgoing deputies plus Michael McGrath (FF), Deirdre Clune (FG), Jerry Buttimer (FG), Ciaran Lynch (Lab), Henry Cremin (SF), Morgan Stack (Ind.), Senator John Minihan (PD)

THE CAMPAIGN: This is another constituency in which Fine Gael will be attempting to win back a seat, in this case, the one lost by Deirdre Clune in 2002. Fianna Fáil's John Dennehy held his seat here then by just six votes, after several recounts, from the Independent Kathy Sinnott, who subsequently was elected to the European Parliament.

Fianna Fáil won three of the seats here in 2002 with almost three quotas. As Michéal Martin had 1.6 quotas, the largest vote in the country, this happened more by accident than design. If they are to hold their three seats in 2007 better vote management will be a must.

This is another of the twenty-three constituencies where Fine

Gael will attempt to reverse the humiliation of five years ago, in 2002 it dropped 11 per cent to just 19 per cent of the vote here. In its favour this time is the voting pact with Labour and the departure of Fianna Fáil's Batt O'Keefe.

Dan Boyle finally made the breakthrough for the Greens in 2002. He's their only deputy who is not Dublin-based. He has to keep ahead of the Labour candidate, Ciaran Lynch, a brother of Kathleen, the Labour deputy for North Central, if he's to retain his seat.

OUR PREDICTION: The only real certainty here is Micheál Martin. Fianna Fáil will win a second seat; a third, though a possibility, might this time prove to be just too difficult. Labour transfers should see the return of two for Fine Gael, most likely, Simon Coveney and Deirdre Clune, and the Green's Dan Boyle.

2 FF, 2 FG, 1 GP. (Fine Gael gain from Fianna Fáil)

CORK SOUTH WEST – THREE SEATS

THE SITTING DEPUTIES: Joe Walsh (FF), Denis O'Donovan (FF), Jim O'Keeffe (FG). Walsh is retiring.

THE CONSTITUENCY: Fine Gael may have had higher profile casualties in 2002, but few of their defeats caused as much shock as Cork South West; PJ Sheehan's demise also serves as a warning to anybody who reckons they can accurately predict what will happen this year because, almost until the end, nobody saw his defeat coming. This, after all, is Michael Collins country.

Cork South West runs from Castletownbere in the west to Kinsale in the east. Among its main towns are Bantry, Bandon and Clonakilty. In the latest boundary review it gains a small amount of territory in the eastern end of the constituency.

Rural issues are always to the fore here. A newly-formed lobby group, the Rural Ireland Alliance, says it aims to place farming and fishing matters at the top of the campaign agenda. The Alliance may run a candidate of its own.

THE LEADING CANDIDATES; O'Donovan and O'Keeffe plus PJ Sheehan (FG), Christy O'Sullivan (FF), Senator Michael McCarthy (Labour), Cionnaith Ó Súilleabháin (SF), Quentin Gargan (Green)

THE CAMPAIGN: In the immediate aftermath of his seat loss, almost nobody expected PJ Sheehan to run for the Dáil again. But, as has been the case at every election since 1969, his name will be on the ballot paper. He also ran in the 2004 local elections, topping the poll in the Bantry electoral area.

Fine Gael frontbencher, Jim O'Keeffe, is also running again. It had been speculated that the party would try and introduce a younger face and Enda Kenny did speak about running a third candidate, but this has now been ruled out.

After an extraordinarily long selection process, Fianna Fáil have also picked two candidates. Denis O'Donovan who topped the poll here last time out after finishing fourth on several occasions will be joined by Christy O'Sullivan. O'Sullivan was a one-time Fianna Fáil member who became an Independent councillor. He also ran as an Independent in 2002 and secured almost 10 per cent of the vote.

His selection caused something of a stir in west Cork politics, with some in Fianna Fáil openly unhappy with the move. Indeed, right up until the day before O'Sullivan's candidacy was announced it was being reported that he was likely to run for the Rural Ireland Alliance.

Michael McCarthy will be running for Labour again after a reasonably strong performance in 2002. This will also be the second general election for Clonakilty town councillor Cionnaith Ó Súilleabháin of Sinn Féin. Quentin Gargan is well known as an environmental campaigner, but this will be his first time as an election candidate.

OUR PREDICTION: Fianna Fail's vote rose only marginally here in 2002, but Fine Gael's vote slumped by 12 per cent. The consencus is that Joe Walsh's retirement will help Enda Kenny's party to regain the upper hand.

There is a view, however, that this could be slightly more complicated than a straight Walsh/Sheehan swap. According to the analysis of some, Cork South West is strongly influenced by geographic trends. There is almost always one TD from the west (currently O'Donovan in Bantry), one from the centre (currently Walsh in Clonakilty) and one from the east (O'Keeffe in Bandon). If that theory were to hold true it would be unlikely that both Sheehan and O'Donovan could both be elected. O'Sullivan (who's based in Clonakilty) or even McCarthy (who's from Dunmanway) would be better placed.

Most local pundits still believe that Fine Gael will get one back here and, while O'Donovan must be favoured to take a seat for Fianna Fáil, those geographic factors mean it is not inconceivable that Christy O'Sullivan could be the victor.

2 FG 1 FF – a gain for Fine Gael from Fianna Fáil.

DONEGAL NORTH EAST – THREE SEATS

OUTGOING DEPUTIES: Jim McDaid (FF), Cecilia Keaveney (FF), Niall Blaney (FF). Niall Blaney was elected as an independent in 2002, but joined Fianna Fáil in 2006.

THE CONSTITUENCY: This three-seat constituency loses part of the area around Raphoe and Lifford, with approximately four and a half thousand votes to Donegal South West. Its main population centres are the towns of Letterkenny, Milford and Buncrana.

Donegal North East has been dominated by political dynasties and larger than life figures for decades.

For eighty years the Blaney family has been a constant force here. Neil Blaney famously broke with Fianna Fáil over the Arms Trial in 1970. Thirty-six years after that rift reconciliation was finally achieved between the Blaney organisation, now led by Niall Blaney TD, and Fianna Fáil.

On the Fine Gael side, Paddy Harte represented Donegal North East for thirty-six years, sensationally losing his seat in 1997.

THE LEADING CANDIDATES: The three outgoing deputies plus Pádraig MacLochlainn (SF), Siobhan McLaughlin (Lab), Frank Gallagher (GP), Councillor Jimmy Harte (Ind), Ian McGarry (Ind), Senator Joe McHugh (FG).

THE CAMPAIGN: The only certainty here is that Fianna Fáil will win one seat. Regional loyalties, internal party divisions and an expected increase in the Sinn Féin vote could well decide how the other two go.

The political geography of Donegal North East is fascinating. The Inishowen peninsula is as big as County Louth and it's got as many voters as County Leitrim. For years Cecilia Keaveney has reigned supreme on the peninsula and with more than 40 per cent of the electorate based here it's unthinkable that they wouldn't return a favourite son or daughter. But expect MacLochlainn of Sinn Féin, who's based in Inishowen, to eat into the Keaveney vote.

In Letterkenny, McDaid and Harte go head to head. While in Milford, Blaney has McHugh as a near neighbour.

The battle within Fianna Fáil will be ferocious. While it's

possible, it's highly unlikely that they can hold the three seats. McDaid originally declared that he was bowing out. Blaney, after protracted negotiations, joined Fianna Fáil. But then out of the blue McDaid changed his mind and decided to run once again. Only a rather temperate acceptance by Blaney of a three-person Fianna Fáil ticket avoided a massive internal party convulsion.

In Fine Gael the decision to go with a single candidate, Joe McHugh, has helped prompt Councillor Jimmy Harte, son of Paddy, to declare as an independent.

OUR PREDICTION: In 2002 the Blaney vote was under 17 per cent; he's seen as the outgoing deputy in greatest jeopardy. While MacLochlainn only managed 40 per cent of a quota last time, the Sinn Féin organisation has strengthened considerably since and even McDaid has predicted that they'll take a seat in both Donegal constituencies. Harte has to be ahead of McHugh on the first count if he's to have any chance. In 2002, with two candidates, Fine Gael got 84 per cent of a quota, so Joe McHugh has a very definite chance to regain the seat held for so long by Paddy Harte. There have been mutterings that the Keaveney seat might come under pressure from either McHugh or MacLochlainn, but with Keaveney and McDaid polling almost 50 per cent of the total vote in 2002, the Fianna Fáil vote would have to collapse if they were to hold only one seat.

The outcome may well be 2 FF with Blaney the likely loser and 1 SF, but McHugh (FG) could upset that prediction.

DONEGAL SOUTH WEST – THREE SEATS

OUTGOING DEPUTIES: Mary Coughlan (FF), Pat 'The Cope' Gallagher (FF), Dinny McGinley (FG).

THE CONSTITUENCY: The principal population centre here

is Donegal town. Killybegs, the largest fishing port in the country, is also here. The 1997 general election produced one of the shock results with the election of Tom Gildea, who campaigned on the issue of the restoration of a television deflector system. Part of the Raphoe area in Donegal North East transfers here.

THE LEADING CANDIDATES: All the outgoing deputies, plus Pearse Doherty (SF) and Sean Ó Maolchallann (GP).

THE CAMPAIGN: This is another of Sinn Féin's target constituencies. Pearse Doherty polled 65,000 votes in the European Elections in 2004, way ahead of the first preference vote of the Fianna Fáil and Fine Gael candidates.

Fianna Fáil have once again Mary Coughlan, the Minister for Agriculture, and Pat 'The Cope' Gallagher as their candidates.

Dinny McGinley is another of those veteran Fine Gael TDs who has been cajoled into standing again, despite having planned to retire. Even with McGinley running again, Fine Gael may have a real battle with Sinn Féin to hold onto the seat.

Sinn Féin claim that tallies taken during the Euro election count showed Doherty polling over 12,000. In the pre-election psychological battle, Jim McDaid, in neighbouring Donegal North East, gave a hostage to fortune, when he predicted Sinn Féin victories in both Donegal constituencies.

OUR PREDICTION: Fine Gael should have a fighting chance. The memory of the Gildea upset in 1997 will ensure that there's no complacency in Fianna Fáil; but if there's any slippage on the 1.68 quotas they got in 2002 they could be in trouble.

2 FF 1 SF (SF gain from FG)

THE ELECTION BOOK

DUBLIN SOUTH WEST – FOUR SEATS

OUTGOING DEPUTIES: Charlie O'Connor (FF), Conor Lenihan (FF), Pat Rabbitte (Lab), Séan Crowe (SF).

THE CONSTITUENCY: The Dublin South West is a four-seater covering the greater Tallaght area from Firhouse to the Naas Road. It gains part of Firhouse with approximately 7,000 votes from Dublin South.

THE LEADING CANDIDATES: The four outgoing deputies plus Senator Brian Hayes (FG), Mick Murphy (SP) and Elizabeth Davidson (GP).

THE CAMPAIGN: All eyes will be on Senator Brian Hayes, the surprise loser in 2002, to see if he can win the seat back for Fine Gael.

In 1997 Hayes, spectacularly topped the poll and none of the political pundits foresaw his demise five years later. In 2002, one of the two Fianna Fáil seats seemed most vulnerable, with Sinn Féin's Séan Crowe widely fancied. Crowe did take a seat, but with the Fianna Fáil vote up 9 per cent and sitting on almost two quotas Charlie O'Connor and Conor Lenihan were comfortably returned. Hayes, whose vote dropped by a third of a quota, was another in the catalogue of Fine Gael casualties. The Labour leader, Pat Rabbitte, has never been a big vote-getter, but he did well in 2002. His vote at over 17 per cent was up 5 percentage points on 1997.

From the perspectives of both Fianna Fáil and Fine Gael, Dublin Southwest is a pivotal constituency. This could well be one of those 'weather vane' constituencies and certainly the omens are that if Brian Hayes doesn't take one of the Fianna Fáil held seats, Enda Kenny can forget any ideas of forming the next government.

OUR PREDICTION: It's most likely that three of the outgoing deputies, Pat Rabbitte, Séan Crowe and either Charlie O'Connor or

Conor Lenihan of Fianna Fáil, will be returned leaving Hayes to battle it out with the remaining Fianna Fáil candidate for the fourth and final seat.

Labour had a good local government election here in 2004. They won four of the ten council seats and only bad vote management deprived them of a fifth seat. This and Rabbitte's enhanced profile as party leader should see an increase in the Labour vote at the general election. The transfer from Rabbitte to Hayes could yet be decisive as to where the last seat goes.

Our prediction: 1 FF, 1 Lab, 1 SF & 1 FG.

DUBLIN CENTRAL – FOUR SEATS

OUTGOING DEPUTIES: Bertie Ahern (FF), Dermot Fitzpatrick (FF), Tony Gregory (Ind), Joe Costello (Lab). Dermot Fitzpatrick is retiring.

THE CONSTITUENCY: Dublin Central's boundaries are the River Liffey to the south, the Phoenix Park to the west, Griffith Avenue to the north and the Drumcondra Road to the east. Dublin Central is the constituency of An Taoiseach Bertie Ahern.

THE LEADING CANDIDATES: All the outgoing deputies, except Dermot Fitzpatrick, plus Mary Fitzpatrick (FF), Senator Cyprian Brady (FF), Mary Lou McDonald (SF), Patricia McKenna (GP), Paschal Donohoe (FG).

THE CAMPAIGN: One of the certainties of the election is that Bertie Ahern will once again be returned here at the top of the poll. He got 32 per cent of the vote in 2002, but whether Fianna Fáil can hold their two seats is another matter. Last time Dermot Fitzpatrick only won his seat by 79 votes from Nicky Kehoe of Sinn Féin. This time MEP Mary Lou McDonald is the Sinn Féin candidate and if she is to take a seat it will be most probably at the expense of either Fianna Fáil or Labour.

The late Jim Mitchell of Fine Gael was a loser here in 2002. If Cllr. Paschal Donohoe, the FG candidate this time, were to improve on the 11 per cent they got last time, it would be hailed as a good day's work.

The decision of former Green MEP Patricia McKenna to run here has meant that not only is Dublin Central one of the most congested constituencies when it comes to political heavyweights, but it is one of the hardest to predict.

There are rumblings that Fianna Fáil may reduce the number of its candidates from three to two; a three person ticket would make it very difficult from them to win two of the four seats. The speculation is rampant as to who the unlucky person might be, Cyprian Brady or Mary Fitzpatrick.

OUR PREDICTION: Just who is or is not Bertie Ahern's running mate could be vital in determining whether Fianna Fáil can hold its two seats. The threat to the second Fianna Fáil seat will come from McKenna and in particular McDonald. Having a woman on the Fianna Fáil ticket just might be the best option for Fianna Fáil if they're to hold the two seats.

Tony Gregory has represented Dublin Central for twenty-five years and his has to be one of the most secure independent seats in the Dáil.

The Labour seat is vulnerable. Joe Costello made it last time, eventually, courtesy of Fine Gael transfers and they could be decisive once again.

1 FF, 1 Lab, 1 Ind, 1 SF. (SF gain from FF).

DUBLIN MID WEST – FOUR SEATS

OUTGOING DEPUTIES: John Curran (FF), Mary Harney

(PD), Paul Gogarty (GP)

THE CONSTITUENCY: Dublin Mid West gains a seat and will now be a four seater. Its two main centres of population are Clondalkin and Lucan and it also includes areas like Newcastle, Saggart, Rathcoole and Brittas. It now gains the Palmerstown area and around seven thousand extra votes from Dublin West.

The two large suburban communities of Clondalkin and Lucan are starkly independent of each other. In Mid West it's a case of being either the Lucan candidate or the Clondalkin one. To illustrate the point the local newspaper, *The Gazette*, even produces separate Lucan and Clondalkin editions.

THE LEADING CANDIDATES: The three outgoing deputies plus Luke Moriarty (FF), Senator Joanna Tuffy (Lab), Joanne Spain (SF), Derek Keating (Ind), Frances Fitzgerald (FG), Mick Finnegan (WP)

THE CAMPAIGN: Most people here expect former Tánaiste and Progressive Democrat leader to be returned and another real certainty is that Fianna Fáil will win one of the four seats here. There'll be a real battle for the remaining two seats with the Greens, Sinn Féin, Fine Gael, Labour and the Independent, Keating, all in the mix. Another candidate from the parties of the Left will be Mick Finnegan of the Worker's Party.

Sinn Féin did well here in the local elections polling almost four thousand first preferences. Surprisingly their Clondalkin based poll-topper, Shane O'Connor, is not the candidate, but twenty-eight-year-old Trinity College graduate, Joanne Spain.

Mid West was another Fine Gael disaster zone in 2002. Outgoing Dublin West deputy, Austin Currie, moved to the new Mid West constituency, but he and running mate Therese Ridge only mustered 11.5 per cent of the vote. This time Fine Gael hopes lie with Frances Fitzgerald, who lost her Dublin South East seat in the same election.

Paul Gogarty of the Green Party with less than half a quota was the surprise here last time out. And this time no one can discount the chances of the independent, Keating. He got nearly 3,700 votes in the local government elections and is campaigning on the so called 'quality of life' issues like public transport, child care and health. If Mid West produces a surprise then Keating is tailor-made.

OUR PREDICTION: Curran should make it for Fianna Fáil, but he can't rest easy with his millionaire running mate Moriarty running a high powered campaign, in which money, apparently, is no object.

Fine Gael is making no bones about the fact that it's the Harney seat they're targeting. It would be one of the shocks of election if Fitzgerald were to succeed in this.

Joanna Tuffy has to be favoured to take a seat but again the Sinn Féin problem with gaining sufficient transfers could be too much for Joanne Spain to surmount. And we could have an intriguing battle between the two Lucan-based candidates Paul Gogarty and Derek Keating. The leading one of this pair is likely to benefit hugely from the transfers of the other.

1 FF, 1 PD, 1 Lab & 1 GP.

DUBLIN NORTH CENTRAL – THREE SEATS

OUTGOING DEPUTIES: Sean Haughey (FF), Ivor Callely (FF), Richard Bruton (FG), Finian McGrath (Ind).

THE CONSTITUENCY: Dublin North Central loses a seat and is now a three-seat constituency. It includes areas such as Marino, Donnycarney and Clontarf. It loses parts of Raheny and Edenmore to Dublin North East and parts of Drumcondra and

Beaumont to Dublin North West, altogether losing about 10,600 votes.

THE LEADING CANDIDATES: The outgoing deputies plus Senator Derek McDowell (Lab), Bronwen Maher (GP), Peter Lawlor (SF).

THE CAMPAIGN: This a case of four into three won't go. With the constituency now reduced to three seats, at least one of the outgoing deputies will not be returning to the Dáil.

This is one of the most cut-throat constituencies in the country. The four outgoing deputies will have serious competition from Labour senator Derek McDowell, who lost his Dáil seat in 2002, and Bronwen Maher of the Green Party. Neither of these can be ruled out.

McGrath, with less than half a quota, pulled off an extraordinary victory in 2002. He'd been contesting elections here since 1989, so he could hardly be described as an overnight success. He has made health, and the plight of special-needs children, his principal political issues.

Both Sean Haughey and Ivor Callely have fearsome reputations as vote-getters. They wiped the floor with the rest of the field five years ago.

Fine Gael dropped 9 per cent in this constituency in the last election. It was a dismal vote, but enough to re-elect Richard Bruton and to put that vote, poor though it was, into context, it was the party's second highest in Dublin.

OUR PREDICTION: Fianna Fáil will take a seat, as will Richard Bruton for Fine Gael; Fianna Fáil have to be strong favourites for the third seat.

If there is to be an upset the chasing pack has to pray for an early Bruton election; if Bruton has to rely on transfers from McDowell, Maher or McGrath, in the event of the elimination of one of them, the potential transfers would be lost to the other two. It's a tall order.

2 FF. 1 FG. (Ind. loss due to boundary change).

DUBLIN NORTH EAST – THREE SEATS

Dublin North East

OUTGOING DEPUTIES: Michael Woods (FF), Martin Brady (FF), Tommy Broughan (Lab).

THE CONSTITUENCY: Dublin North East was a four seat constituency until 2002. It contains suburbs like Donaghmede, Artane and Sutton. It gains the Edenmore and Woodbine areas from Dublin North Central, with about 4,000 votes.

THE LEADING CANDIDATES: Brody Sweeney (FG), Terence Flanagan (FG), Tommy Broughan (Lab), Larry O'Toole (SF), David Healy (GP), Keith Redmond (PD).

At the time of going to press Fianna Fáil still hadn't finalised their ticket. It's expected that their two outgoing deputies, Michael Woods and Martin Brady, will be their candidates.

THE CAMPAIGN: Michael Woods, who was first elected in 1977, still hasn't publicly declared whether he is running or not. This has caused considerable frustration and annoyance, particularly, amongst the supporters of Senator Liam Fitzgerald, who lost his Dáil seat to Martin Brady in 1997, and Councillor Tom Brabazon. Both Fitzgerald and Brabazon have openly declared their aspirations to be Fianna Fáil candidates.

Martin Brady will be a candidate, but if Woods decides to go again there's a very real possibility that his thirty-year-long Dáil career could end in defeat.

The main threat to one of the Fianna Fáil seat comes from Sinn Féin. Their candidate, Councillor Larry O'Toole, has been steadily building up a power base here. In the local elections O'Toole, in the Artane ward, and Killian Forde, in the Donaghmede ward, both topped the poll, with almost 8,000 votes between them, more than a quota in the last general election.

Fine Gael too have to be in the mix for that third seat. They have a solid and well-balanced ticket, with Councillor Terence Flanagan from Artane and Brody Sweeney, the MD of the O'Brien's sandwich shop chain. Sweeney has been operating a full-time campaign for over a year. It would be a massive boost for Fine Gael, nationally, if they were to regain the seat lost by Michael Joe Cosgrave in 2002.

Labour won two seats here back in 1992 and no one really expects Tommy Broughan not to be in the next Dáil.

While the Green Party candidate, David Healy, is expected to increase the party vote, it would be a major surprise if he took a seat.

OUR PREDICTION: Fianna Fáil are certainties for one seat. The rise of Sinn Féin in the constituency, a vigorous Fine Gael campaign and the uncertainty and frustration caused by the apparent indecision in finalising are all factors which could contribute to Fianna Fáil dropping a seat. Tommy Broughan should make it, leaving Fianna Fáil, Fine Gael and Sinn Féin to battle it out for the final seat. 1 FF, 1 Lab, 1 SF, (SF gain from FF).

DUBLIN NORTH WEST – THREE SEATS

OUTGOING DEPUTIES: Noel Ahern (FF), Pat Carey (FF), Roisin Shortall (Lab)

THE CONSTITUENCY: There have been two slight boundary changes to Dublin North West since the last general election. The more significant of these is the addition of part of the

Whitehall-Beaumont area.

This is a largely working-class constituency, consisting mainly of the suburbs of Finglas and Ballymun and parts of Glasnevin. Some of the constituency remains blighted by disadvantage and drugs. The Ballymun Regeneration Programme is gradually improving the area, the infamous towers are being torn down and new houses put in their place, but locals say it still has a long way to go. In neighbouring Finglas, a number of horrific killings – including the murder of an innocent bystander, Anthony Campbell – have highlighted the extent of gangland crime. People who live here say there is also a problem with more petty crime, and with anti-social behaviour. Heroin has claimed a significant number of young lives in Dublin North West over the past two decades. Those working to combat drug addiction say cocaine is also a growing problem.

On a more positive note, there has been a rise in employment in the constituency.

THE LEADING CANDIDATES: In addition to the three sitting deputies, Dr Bill Tormey (FG), Dessie Ellis (SF), John Dunne (WP), Owen Martin (WP)

THE CAMPAIGN: The may do so grudgingly, but almost everybody you speak to believes that Noel – brother of Bertie – Ahern will be re-elected. The Minister of State with special responsibility for housing and drugs strategy was elected on his first attempt in 1992 and has headed the poll on the last two occasions. His vote is based largely in the Glasnevin part of the constituency.

The majority view has it that Roisin Shortall will also be returning to Leinster House with the assistance of transfers from Fine Gael's Dr Bill Tormey. This will be the Beaumont consultant's sixth general election. On the first two occasions, he ran for Labour and on the subsequent three as an Independent. He joined Fine Gael prior to the last local elections and, by winning a seat on Dublin City Council, tasted electoral success for the first time. He sees this is a good portent for the General Election. It must be said, however, that last time out his vote and the Fine Gael vote combined still fell well short of that achieved by Roisin Shortall.

The main question in Dublin North West is whether Dessie Ellis of Sinn Féin can take a seat. On the last occasion, the Finglas man took 18 per cent of the first preference vote, outpolling Shortall. But he did so poorly on transfers that he ended up more than a thousand votes behind the Labour TD. He polled very strongly at the subsequent local elections, taking almost 30 per cent of the Finglas vote.

Sinn Féin are confident that they can take a Dáil seat on this occasion. If they do, the most likely loser is Pat Carey. Fianna Fáil are equally adamant that their man will hold on. Local observers say he has certainly been putting in a massive effort. One expressed the view that if the general election was held three years ago, Dessie Ellis would have been an absolute cert, but that things have changed in the meantime.

OUR PREDICTION: Nearly all of Dublin's constituencies are difficult to call, and this one is no exception. Following on from his massive vote in 2004, though, Ellis must be the slight favourite.

1 FF , 1 Lab, 1 SF.

DUBLIN NORTH – FOUR SEATS

SITTING DEPUTIES: Trevor Sargent (Green), Jim Glennon (FF), GV Wright (FF), Seán Ryan (Lab) Glennon, Wright and Ryan are retiring.

THE CONSTITUENCY: In common with most east coast

constituencies, Dublin North has seen a massive increase in population since the start of the century. Between 2002 and 2006, the population grew by 21 per cent, putting it second only to Dublin West in terms of the number of people per TD. Indeed, the constituency of Dún Laoghaire now has a smaller population than Dublin North, but has five seats.

The building surge has been particularly pronounced in the Balbriggan area, in Swords and in Lusk. For instance, the preliminary census figures show that in just four years the population of the Balbriggan rural electoral division more than doubled and the population of Swords-Lissenhall grew by 50 per cent. Also in this constituency are areas such as Malahide, Portmarnock, Rush and Lusk. All the parties are agreed that this phenomenal rate of growth makes it harder to predict how people will vote in the General Election.

There has been a slight boundary change since the last election with approximately 4,000 people in the St Margaret's / Kilsallaghan area being moved into Dublin West.

Large numbers commute into Dublin city centre every day, so issues such as traffic and public transport are high on the voters' agenda here. Another familiar problem is a lack of school places. But this is also the Dublin Airport constituency, and for several elections now questions over the future of jobs at Aer Lingus have been prominent in the campaign. The same can be expected this time.

THE LEADING CANDIDATES: Trevor Sargent (GP), Joe Corr (GP), Michael Kennedy (FF), John O'Leary (FF), Daragh O'Brien (FF), Dr James Reilly (FG), Brendan Ryan (Lab), Clare Daly (SP), Tom Morrissey (PD), Matt McCormack (SF), David O'Connor (Ind.)

THE CAMPAIGN: There is only one thing that can be said for

sure about Dublin North. Trevor Sargent will be elected. This will be the Green Party leader's sixth General Election. He has been returned on every occasion since 1992, and in 2002 he topped the poll. This will be the first time he has a running mate. The Greens' second candidate is Joe Corr, who is a member of Fingal County Council and, like Trevor Sargent, is based in the Balbriggan area. If there was a huge swing to the Greens on polling day there is an outside chance that they could take a second seat, but the party is probably more focused on the election after next when this is likely to be a five-seat constituency.

For years, Ray Burke was Fianna Fáil's top man in Dublin North. Despite the departure of both of their sitting TDs, it is also highly likely that the party will take at least one seat here. They got 38 per cent of the vote in 2002, a slight fall on the previous election. The candidate who failed to get elected last time out, Michael Kennedy, a Swords-based member of Fingal county council, will be running again. Kennedy was also an unsuccessful candidate in the 1998 by-election that followed Ray Burke's resignation. A first-time candidate will be the former Dublin gaelic football goalkeeper, John O'Leary.

Few will have forgotten the emotional scenes at the Dublin North count in 2002 when Nora Owen realised that she had lost her seat. Because the votes had been cast and counted electronically, the former Justice Minister had no fore-warning of her defeat. In the event, it presaged a catastrophic weekend for her party. Opinion is divided as to whether Fine Gael will make a comeback on this occasion. The party is running just one candidate, Dr James Reilly who is a former President of the Irish Medical Organisation.

The dark horse here is Tom Morrissey of the Progessive Democrats. This will be the first time his name will feature on the

Dublin North ballot paper, but he's not lacking in experience. He was the PD candidate in Dublin West in two general elections, and represented Fine Gael in that constituency in an earlier general election and a by-election. He is currently one of the Taoiseach's appointments in the Seanad. There was no PD candidate in this constituency at the last election. Tom Morrissey may not win a seat himself, but he could take votes from Fine Gael and stymie that party's attempted comeback.

It's safe to predict that no matter what the final outcome there will be a fair degree of interest in the performance of Clare Daly of the Socialist Party. This will be her third general election and she was the last remaining unelected candidate in 2002. Two years later she topped the poll in the Swords electoral area of Fingal County Council. Her critics say that the Dublin Airport-based SIPTU shop steward is over-reliant on the Swords area for her support. She argues she has been working throughout the constituency and hopes to get a substantial vote in many of the newer estates.

OUR PREDICTION: Trevor Sargent is favourite to top the poll and be elected with relative ease, but almost everybody you speak to will propose a different combination of candidates for the remaining three seats. There will undoubtedly be at least one Fianna Fáil seat, and Michael Kennedy appears to be best-placed. Clare Daly was almost there in 2002 and should go one better on this occasion.

But if Daly is elected is it really possible that Brendan Ryan could also take a seat? And what about Fine Gael? On the plus side they once held two seats out of three in Dublin North. But that was more than twenty years ago, they have a lot of ground to make up and Tom Morrissey is biting at their heels. Is it likely then that Fianna Fáil will hold on to two seats despite both of their incumbents retiring? Or if the Green Party are having a really good day, could Joe Corr sneak in?

Dublin North is one of those constituencies where no prediction can be made with any huge conviction. A significant amount will depend on the overall trend on polling day. On 'The Constituency', Gene McKenna of the *Irish Independent* opted for Dr James Reilly of Fine Gael. We'll stick with that prediction. But it could, just as easily, be Fianna Fáil or Labour.

DUBLIN SOUTH CENTRAL – FIVE SEATS

THE SITTING DEPUTIES: Sean Ardagh (FF), Michael Mulcahy (FF), Gay Mitchell (FG), Mary Upton (Lab), Aengus Ó Snodaigh (SF). Gay Mitchell was elected to the European Parliament in 2004 and won't be contesting the general election.

THE CONSTITUENCY: According to the 2006 census figures, 122,000 people live in Dublin South Central, making it the capital's most populous constituency. Encompassing areas such as Ballyfermot, Crumlin, Inchicore and Walkinstown it has long been seen as a largely working-class constituency. But, as always, things are a little more complex than that. Parts of the constituency are largely middle-class and other parts, especially the inner-city flats complexes, are home to some of the most disadvantaged people in the country. They are also the most disenfranchised. In 2002 the turnout here was lower than anywhere else. Only 52 per cent of those registered to vote did so. Even accounting for the shambolic state of the electoral register, this is an exceptionally low figure, which should worry all of those involved in politics.

The constituency boundaries have been changed slightly since the last election. Dublin South Central gains a small amount of territory around the Islandbridge area from Dublin Central.

THE LEADING CANDIDATES: All of the sitting TDs apart from Gay Mitchell plus Catherine Byrne (FG), Anne Marie Martin (FG), Eric Byrne (Lab), Tony McDermott (GP), Brid Smith (People Before Profit Alliance), Andrew McGuinness (WP), Joan Collins (Ind)

THE CAMPAIGN: It has been widely acknowledged that Gay Mitchell's decision to stay in Brussels is a blow for Fine Gael. In the first instance, the party has lost a proven vote-getter. Although he didn't top the poll in 2002, he was first elected. That was some achievement on a day when Fine Gael were being all but annihilated in Dublin. Secondly, if Enda Kenny is Taoiseach come this summer, Gay Mitchell would have been a shoo-in for a place in cabinet. So his decision has been seen by some as a vote of no confidence in his party's election prospects.

The rumour machine had it that another member of the extended Mitchell family would be on the ballot paper instead. That didn't come to pass and Fine Gael's two candidates will be Catherine Byrne and Anne Marie Martin. A former Lord Mayor, Byrne also ran in 2002, but was well down the field. Martin was co-opted onto Dublin City Council in Gay Mitchell's place in 2003. She was re-elected for the Crumlin-Kimmage ward the following yea, but with a substantially smaller vote than her predecesor.

Aengus Ó Snodaigh more than doubled the Sinn Féin vote here in 2002 and gained a seat for his party. It would be a big surprise if he wasn't re-elected.

Mary Upton will again be joined on the Labour ticket by city councillor, Eric Byrne. First elected for the Workers Party in 1989, he has had a varied electoral career. As a member of Democratic Left, he lost the seat at the next election following a week of counting and recounting. Two years later he returned to the Dáil following a by-election. In 1997 he was gone again. In 2002, and by now a Labour candidate, he also narrowly lost out. He is certainly a serious contender on this occasion and he argues that he could be the main beneficiary of Gay Mitchell's departure.

Despite speculation that they would have three candidates, Fianna Fáil have decided to stick with their two sitting TDs. Sean Ardagh has been a TD since 1997 and topped the poll five years ago. Michael Mulcahy had contested two general elections and two by-elections before finally becoming entering the Dáilat the last election.

A year ago, few would have considered the Green Party representative, Tony McDermott, to be a serious contender here. But if the party's standing in Dublin is as strong as several opinion polls have suggested, he can't be ruled out. McDermott is a member of South Dublin County Council for the Terenure/Rathfarnham electoral area and this will be his first general election.

Another candidate who is being tipped to put in a relatively strong performance is the Independent, Joan Collins. Three years ago she became a member of Dublin City Council. She was elected largely on an anti-service charges platform, and has also campaigned on a range of other community issues.

The Progressive Democrats say they may have a candidate, but have yet to announce a name.

OUR PREDICTION: The consensus has it that three candidates – Sean Ardagh, Aengus Ó Snodaigh and Mary Upton – are ahead of the rest of the field and shouldn't have too much to worry about. After that it gets ferociously competitive. Local observers say that a string of candidates are in the frame for the remaining two seats. Those mentioned are Michael Mulcahy, Eric Byrne, the stronger of the two Fine Gael women, Tony McDermott and Joan Collins. It should be said, however, that much of this speculation is based on the most dubious of sources – private opinion polls conducted by the larger parties.

At a national level Fine Gael are likely to see their vote improve on 2002 but they could be squeezed out in Dublin South Central. Having said that, Michael Mulcahy's vote is also seen as pretty shaky.

As with many constituencies, the final outcome will be highly dependent on the national trends in the weeks immediately prior to polling and Tony McDermott could pull off a big surprise. But we'll go for Mulcahy to hold on, Fine Gael to lose out and Eric Byrne to scrape in.

That would leave it 2 FF, 2 Lab, 1 SF – a gain for Labour from Fine Gael

DUBLIN SOUTH EAST – FOUR SEATS

OUTGOING DEPUTIES: Michael McDowell (PD), Eoin Ryan (FF), Ruairi Quinn (Lab), John Gormley (GP).

THE CONSTITUENCY: Dublin South East includes middle-class areas like Sandymount, Ballsbridge, Ranelagh and Donnybrook along with working-class areas like Ringsend and the south inner city. It's the constituency of the Tánaiste and PD leader, Michael McDowell, and Ruairi Quinn, former leader of the Labour Party.

THE LEADING CANDIDATES: Eoin Ryan (FF) was elected to the European Parliament and will not be contesting the general election, leaving the three other outgoing deputies plus Lucinda Creighton (FG), Chris Andrews (FF), Jim O'Callaghan (FF), Daithí Doolan (SF).

THE CAMPAIGN: This is another constituency in which Fine Gael has high hopes of regaining the seat Frances Fitzgerald lost in

2002. Then, the constituency once represented by Garret FitzGerald, saw the Fine Gael vote plummet by eleven per cent. Councillor Lucinda Creighton, who has risen through the ranks of the Fine Gael youth organisation, has a mammoth task on her hands. Much of the old Fine Gael vote here has very obviously moved to that party's former member, Michael McDowell. Neither of the Fianna Fáil candidates, Chris Andrews, son of former TD and MEP, the late Niall Andrews, or barrister, Jim O'Callaghan, could manage to get elected in the 2004 council elections. In spite of highly optimistic Fine Gael suggestions some time ago, that Fianna Fáil could end up without a seat here, the Fianna Fáil vote, which was 27 per cent in 2002, would have to collapse for that to happen. In the 2002 contest many expected a repeat of the titanic struggle between McDowell and Gormley five years earlier. The Green Party candidate then eventually pipped McDowell for the last seat, after a week of recounts. Last time though, both were elected comfortably, with McDowell topping the poll. It would be a major upset if either were to lose. Ruairi Quinn only made it in 2002 with less than 12 per cent of the vote, but there is a formidable Labour Party machine here that should ensure his return to Leinster House. Sinn Féin's Daithí Doolan is based in the south inner city. He could be a contender for a seat if there is a big national swing to his party, but realistically he is very much the outsider in this race.

OUR PREDICTION: Even on a bad day Fianna Fáil should hold its seat. McDowell may again be the poll topper, but no PD deputy can ever take anything for granted, and he has twice lost his seat here before. Quinn and Gormley, helped possibly by transfers from Sinn Féin, should again make it.

1 FF, 1 PD, 1 Lab and 1 GP. (No change).

DUBLIN SOUTH – FIVE SEATS

OUTGOING DEPUTIES: Seamus Brennan (FF), Tom Kitt (FF), Liz O'Donnell (PD), Olivia Mitchell (FG), Eamon Ryan (GP).

THE CONSTITUENCY: Dublin South includes middle-class suburbs like Stillorgan, Dundrum, Sandyford and Churchtown. It stretches from the Dodder river to the foothills of the Dublin mountains. For this election it loses about a thousand houses in the Firhouse to Dublin South West.

THE LEADING CANDIDATES: The five outgoing deputies plus Maria Corrigan (FF), Alan Shatter (FG), Jim O'Leary (FG), Aidan Culhane (Lab), Alex White (Lab), Shaun Tracey (SF), Sorcha Nic Cormaic (SF).

THE CAMPAIGN: The big story in 2002 was the loss of the seat of Fine Gael's long serving TD and frontbencher Alan Shatter to Eamon Ryan of the Greens. Dublin South is high on Fine Gael's target list and the seat in their sights is the PD one, held since 1992 by Liz O'Donnell. Liz is one of politics' great survivors with fifteen years unbroken service in the Dáil despite her party's ups and downs.

It's not just Fine Gael targeting the O'Donnell seat, Labour also have a chance in this constituency; back in 1992, Eithne Fitzgerald of the Labour party got a remarkable 17,000 first preferences here, and in 2002 she got almost 10 per cent of the vote. However, if either of the current Labour candidates, Alex White or Aidan Culhane, were to take a seat it could well be that of the 2002 surprise packet, Eamon Ryan of the Greens.

Dublin South has always returned high-profile candidates and every one of its five deputies here are of ministerial calibre.

The Fianna Fáil vote dipped slightly in 2002, but both Tom Kitt and Seamus Brennan should make it again. Both Olivia Mitchell and Eamon Ryan, with high national profiles, should also be re-elected leaving a battle for the last seat between Liz O'Donnell, Labour and Fine Gael.

If Fine Gael were to wrest a seat back, Jim O'Leary, a councillor based in Stillorgan, could spring a surprise over the more fancied Shatter. Both White and Culhane of Labour are working the constituency assiduously. Maybe this time, Liz O'Donnell just might have used up all her political lives.

OUR PREDICTION: 2FF, 1FG, 1 GP, 1PD

DUBLIN WEST – THREE SEATS

OUTGOING DEPUTIES: Brian Lenihan (FF), Joe Higgins (SP), Joan Burton (Lab).

THE CONSTITUENCY: Dublin West encompasses Blanchardstown, Castleknock and Mulhuddart. For this election it loses Palmerstown, with about 7,000 votes, to Dublin Mid West and gains areas around The Ward and St Margaret's from Dublin North. The population here has increased by 25 per cent since 2002.

THE LEADING CANDIDATES: The three sitting deputies along with Leo Varadkar (FG), Gerry Lynam (FF), Roderic O'Gorman (GP), Felix Gallagher (SF) and Mags Murray (PD)

THE CAMPAIGN: The battle for the three seats here is between the three outgoing deputies and Varadkar of Fine Gael.

Varadkar, a doctor in Crumlin Children's Hospital whose father is a GP in Castleknock, was the runaway winner in Castleknock in the 2004 local elections. His 4,894 first preferences vote, almost two quotas, was the highest recorded in the country. The Fine Gael candidate in 2002, Sheila Terry, performed creditably but was eventually pipped by Joan Burton for the third seat. In 2007, Varadkar is being hailed as Fine Gael's banker in the Dublin constituencies.

For Fianna Fáil, Brian Lenihan, will almost certainly win a seat, but Socialist Party leader, Joe Higgins, comfortably returned in 2002 with 21.5 per cent of the vote, can take nothing for granted. Once again, Joan Burton will be fighting for her political life.

Lenihan, Higgins and Burton are three of the Dáil's outstanding performers who combine high national profiles with acknowledged hardworking attention to their constituency.

Varadkar, hugely ambitious with a populous streak, goes into this campaign on the back of that massive 2004 vote. Whether that was a flash in the pan that won't be so easily repeated against political heavyweights like the incumbents here, we'll just have to wait and see.

A crucial factor in deciding where the third seat goes could be who benefits most from the 2370 votes of the PDs Tom Morrisey in 2002 – Morrisey is not a candidate here this time.

OUR PREDICTION: 1 FF, 1 SP & 1 Lab.

DÚN LAOGHAIRE – FIVE SEATS

SITTING DEPUTIES: Mary Hanafin (FF), Barry Andrews (FF), Eamon Gilmore (Lab), Fiona O'Malley (PD), Ciarán Cuffe (GP)

THE CONSTITUENCY: Of all of Fine Gael's 2002 disasters, Dún Laoghaire must have been one of the most unexpected. In advance of the election, even the most downbeat assessments didn't foresee the party ending up without a seat in the constituency of former Taoiseach, Liam Cosgrave. In the event, that was just what happened. Michael Noonan's party lost two seats – one to the PDs, the other to the Greens. And it was results such as this which ensured that Dublin turned into an electoral wasteground for Fine Gael. The Capital has 47 Dáil seats. Fine Gael hold just three of them.

Dún Laoghaire is a largely middle-class constituency which includes areas such as Blackrock, Foxrock, Killiney and Shankhill. It includes places of phenomenal wealth and pockets of distinct disadvantage. According to the 2006 census figures, it also has the lowest number of people per TD.

THE LEADING CANDIDATES: The sitting deputies plus Sean Barrett (FG), Eugene Regan (FG), John Bailey (FG), Oisín Quinn (Lab), Eoin Ó Broin (SF), Richard Boyd Barrett (People Before Profit Alliance)

THE CAMPAIGN: There is recent precedent for an education minister being unseated here. The then minister, Niamh Breathnach of the Labour Party, failed to be elected in 1997. There aren't many, however, who would argue that the current minister will suffer the same fate. Even her opponents acknowledge that Mary Hanafin is a diligent constituency worker. Although Fianna Fáil's vote may well slip a bit (the party had just over 30 per cent last time out), she is unlikely to be a casualty.

If Fine Gael can't win back a seat here, they are looking at another bleak, bleak day. This was once prime Fine Gael territory. In one of the Garret Fitgerald-era elections, they won three out of the five seats. It is widely acknowledged that last time out their campaign was a shambles. They weren't helped by the fact that both of their sitting TDs – Sean Barrett and Monica Barnes – retired. The party's share of the vote halved – from 31 per cent in 1997 to 15 per cent last time out.

Sean Barrett, a former minister, is back this time. There are two other Fine Gael candidates. Dún Laoghaire-Rathdown councillor,

Eugene Regan, was picked along with Barrett at a selection convention. The former chairman of the Dublin County GAA Board, John Bailey, was later added to the ticket. He was one of the unsuccessful candidates in 2002, but recovered to top the poll in the last local elections. Given that a three-candidate strategy proved so disastrous on that occasion, some eyebrows have been raised by the fact that the party is pursuing the same strategy this time.

Eamon Gilmore will be partnered on the Labour ticket by Oisín Quinn. A nephew of the party leader, Ruairi Quinn, he is a member of Dublin City Council so his base his actually outside this constituency. Labour insiders insist that he will be in the hunt for the last seat.

The big victors in 2002, Fiona O'Malley of the PDs and Ciarán Cuffe of the Greens, will be seeking re-election. Back in 2002, O'Malley, in particular, caused a lot of pundits to eat their words. Given little chance, she took the third seat.

If Fine Gael are to take back a seat, however, somebody will have to lose out. A year ago there was a view that the loser could be Ciarán Cuffe. Every opinion poll indicates, however, that the Green Party are flying in Dublin. So, despite the fact that she does have a good reputation for constituency work, O'Malley's is the name most frequently mentioned. There are also those who argue that Fianna Fail's Barry Andrews might be vulnerable to a Fine Gael-comeback, but that appears to be a minority view.

OUR PREDICTION: Every candidate hates to hear this, but Mary Hanafin and Eamon Gilmore should have little to worry about. Ciarán Cuffe should also make it back to Leinster House. To many outsiders, Fine Gael have made this more difficult for themselves by running three candidates. On balance, however, they must be favourites to take a seat. John Bailey appears to be best positioned of the three, but Sean Barrett won seven general elections in this constituency and can't be ruled out. Fiona O'Malley has proved everybody wrong before, but she could be in trouble. A gain for Fine Gael from the Progressive Democrats.

2FF, 1FG, 1 Lab, 1 GP

GALWAY EAST – FOUR SEATS

OUTGOING DEPUTIES: Noel Treacy (FF), Joe Callanan (FF), Paul Connaughton (FG), Paddy McHugh (Ind.).

THE CONSTITUENCY: This large four-seater stretches from the River Shannon across to Lough Corrib, and from the Mayo border in the north to the Clare border in the south. It includes large towns like Tuam, Ballinasloe, Portumna and Loughrea.

THE LEADING CANDIDATES: The four outgoing deputies plus Senator Micheál Kitt (FF), Senator Ulick Burke (FG), Dr John Barton (FG), Tom McHugh (FG), Ciaran Cannon (PD), Jason Devlin (SF), Colm Keaveney (Lab).

THE CAMPAIGN: This is another constituency in which Fine Gael is going all out to regain the seat it lost in 2002. The then sitting deputy, Ulick Burke, lost to the Independent, Paddy McHugh, from Tuam, who ran after he failed to get a Fianna Fáil nomination. It's fair to say that three of the four seats here are accounted for; two for Fianna Fáil and one for Fine Gael. Election 2007 will find Paddy McHugh battling to hold his seat against the concerted efforts of both Fianna Fáil and Fine Gael.

Fine Gael admit that its strategy in running a four-man ticket is a high-risk one, but believe that Barton, a highly-respected consultant in Portiuncula Hospital in Ballinasloe, can deliver new personal votes, and running Councillor Tom McHugh, from Tuam, going head to head with his namesake, the incumbent

Paddy McHugh, a fellow Tuam man, will eat into the independent's support base. All heady stuff and a real coup if it is pulled off!

Fianna Fáil will have its own internal contest. Junior minister Noel Treacy must be favourite to be returned, but there is a strong chance that Micheál Kitt could regain his Dáil seat at the expense of his party colleague Joe Callanan.

If Fine Gael is to win back its seat, the transfers of Tuam-based Colm Keaveney of Labour could prove to be vital. Keaveney didn't run in 2002, but in 1997, in a constituency with no real Labour Party tradition, he polled 3,500 votes.

OUR PREDICTION: 2 FF, 2 FG (Fine Gael gain from Independent).

GALWAY WEST – FIVE SEATS

OUTGOING DEPUTIES: Eamon Ó Cuiv (FF), Frank Fahey (FF), Padraic McCormack (FG), Michael D. Higgins (Lab), Noel Grealish (PD).

THE CONSTITUENCY: Lough Corrib acts as the boundary between Galway West and Galway East. The constituency stretches north to the Mayo border and south to the border with Clare.

Bobby Molloy, first of Fianna Fáil, and more latterly of the PDs, was ever present here since 1965, before stepping down at the 2002 election. Michael D. Higgins of Labour is another long-standing deputy, who first stood in 1969.

THE LEADING CANDIDATES: All the five outgoing deputies plus Michael Crowe (FF), Sean Kyne (FG), Fidelma Healy Eames (FG), Donal Lyons (PD), Thomas Welby (PD), Niall Ó Brolcháin (GP), Ann Marie Carroll (SF), Catherine Connolly (Ind).

THE CAMPAIGN: Eamon Ó Cuiv of Fianna Fáil is the only one of the outgoing deputies who can feel reasonably secure. Noel Grealish of the Progressive Democrats, who pulled off a sensational win in 2002, has to be the most vulnerable.

The most obvious threat to the status quo comes from the Green Party's Niall Ó Brolcháin, who is currently the mayor of Galway city. If the Greens are to take a seat here it could be at the expense of either the PDs, Labour or Fine Gael.

Internal problems within Labour have caused Cllr. Catherine Connolly, one of four Labour councillors in the city, to leave the party and run as an independent. She'll undoubtedly eat into the Higgins vote, though the expectation is that the lion's share of her second preferences will transfer to him.

Fine Gael too have had their difficulties. Padraic McCormack had decided to retire, but was cajoled by Enda Kenny to reverse his decision and run again.

The question that will dominate this campaign is whether the PDs can repeat their 2002 success. Then, their masterstroke, engineered by Bobby Molloy, to run three candidates, proved to be a winner. Noel Grealish, helped undoubtedly by some Fianna Fáil votes, eventually was elected at the fifteenth count.

OUR PREDICTION: Fianna Fáil will win two seats, most probably Ó Cuiv and Fahey. There's always been a Fine Gael seat in Galway West, and really if they could manage to hold on in 2002, in spite of a 5 point drop in their vote, and on a day of national collapse, they should also retain their seat.

Michael D. Higgins can take nothing for granted. He'll be damaged by his former party colleague Connolly, and Ó Brolcháin and Sinn Féin's Carroll may also take votes from him. Higgins should be the recipient of sufficient transfers to see him through though.

We then could have the prospect of a head-to-head battle for the last seat between the Greens and the PDs. Noel Grealish is buttressed by two known vote-getters in Lyons and Welby, but whether the old Molloy machine is as strong as it once was, we'll have to wait and see.

Ó Brolcháin's chances are certainly being enhanced by national media attention, and being the current mayor of Galway can't be a hindrance either. His 2002 vote was unspectacular, but he did hold on until the thirteenth count, attracting transfers from all over the place.

It's really anybody's guess as to where that fifth seat goes. How the national mood blows could be decisive.

2 FF, 1 FG, 1 Lab, 1 GP (GP gain from PD)

KERRY NORTH – THREE SEATS

OUTGOING DEPUTIES: Tom McEllistrim (FF), Jimmy Deenihan (FG), Martin Ferris (SF).

THE CONSTITUENCY: Tralee is the principal population centre. Kerry North was represented continuously from 1943 until 2002 by first, Dan Spring, and then his son Dick. The former of the Labour party lost his seat to Martin Ferris of Sinn Fein in 2002.

In Fianna Fáil, Tom McEllistrim is the third generation of his family to have represented the constituency since 1923.

THE LEADING CANDIDATES: The outgoing deputies plus Norma Foley (FF), Terry O'Brien (Lab), David Grey (GP), Sean Locke (Ind), Anthony Dineen (Ind).

THE CAMPAIGN: Much of the focus here will be on the battle by Labour to win back the seat that they sensationally lost to Sinn Féin in 2002. It's no secret that Sinn Féin views the Martin Ferris seat as probably their most vulnerable of the six that they currently hold. Labour are all out for revenge, and in Councillor Terry O'Brien they have a real chance. O'Brien, who was a polltopper in the local elections in Tralee, has been confined to a wheelchair for the past eighteen years, following an accident in a swimming pool.

Tom McEllistrim hasn't exactly set the world on fire since his election, but with Norma Foley, a daughter of former TD Denis, making up the Fianna Fáil team, they should retain the Fianna Fáil seat comfortably.

In 2002 Jimmy Deenihan benefited from the transfers of the Fianna Fáil candidate, Dan Kiely, who came from the same part of the constituency, to get elected. This time he's got the northern end of the constituency to himself. Without the prospect of significant transfers he could be in trouble.

OUR PREDICTION: Fianna Fáil will win one seat. Then we'll be left with the three into two conundrum. Will it be Deenihan, Ferris or O'Brien who takes the other two? It's anyone's guess.

O'Brien, helped by his location in Tralee, should make it. Dick Spring had 90 per cent of a quota in 2002, and O'Brien can expect a much greater share of transfers from eliminated candidates, who are all based in the Tralee area, than Fine Gael's Jimmy Deenihan, who's base is in Lixnawe, at the northern end of the constituency.

Before Martin Ferris arrived on the scene, Kerry North was an easy prediction. One seat each to Fianna Fáil, Fine Gael and Labour. That all changed in 2002, and we could have another upset here this time. The casualty might be Deenihan rather than Ferris. 1 FF, 1 Lab, 1 SF.

KERRY SOUTH – THREE SEATS

OUTGOING DEPUTIES: John O'Donoghue (FF), Breeda Moynihan Cronin (Lab), Jackie Healy-Rae (Ind).

THE CONSTITUENCY: Large towns here include Killarney and Killorglin.

THE LEADING CANDIDATES: The outgoing deputies plus Tom Fleming (FF), Séamus Cosaí Fitzgerald (FG), Tom Sheehan (FG).

THE CAMPAIGN: The two big questions here are, can Fianna Fáil win back the seat taken by their former stalwart, Jackie Healy-Rae in 1997, and can Fine Gael win back the seat from Labour that they last held in 1981.

Fianna Fáil pushed up their vote by almost 13 per cent last time on their 1997 showing, and certainly a little extra push could get them that seat; they only missed out by 203 votes.

Jackie Healy-Rae is of course the man that Fianna Fáil have in their sights. He had a narrow squeak in 2002, but there are suggestions, that some of his less ardent supporters drifted back to Fianna Fáil, in the belief that his seat was safe. He has two sons sitting as councillors and an acknowledged formidable political machine; there doesn't appear to be any great rush to pen the Healy-Rae political obituary, just yet.

Breeda Moynihan Cronin decided last year not to seek re-election. This seemed to provide Fine Gael with a golden opportunity to win back the seat that they once held, all those years ago, by Michael Begley. Those hopes were greatly dampened by the news that Breeda Moynihan Cronin has changed her mind and is once more a candidate.

OUR PREDICTION: The only thing definite here is that Fianna Fáil will win one seat. The Fine Gael decision, to once again field two candidates, will probably work to Moynihan Cronin's advantage, with the Fine Gael vote split. Whether Jackie Healy-Rae is returned or not won't greatly affect the political complexion of the next Dáil, as he votes solidly with Fianna Fail. 1 FF, 1 Lab, 1 Ind (no change).

KILDARE NORTH – FOUR SEATS

SITTING DEPUTIES: Bernard Durkan (FG), Emmett Stagg (Lab), Catherine Murphy (Ind.). Charlie McCreevy (FF) was elected in 2002, but resigned his seat to take up the position of Ireland's EU Commissioner. Catherine Murphy won the by-election held in March 2005

THE CONSTITUENCY: Kildare North gets an extra seat and is also gaining some territory in the north west of the county from Kildare South. The census figures showed that the overall population of Kildare North had risen by 10 per cent between 2002 and 2006.

Following Charlie McCreevy's departure for Brussels and Fianna Fáil's by-election defeat, this is the only constituency in the state with no Fianna Fáil TD. Politicos on all sides agree that the by-election campaign, and the focus on commuter and suburban issues, had some impact on the national political agenda. It was no surprise, say locals, that childcare was at the heart of Brian Cowen's next budget.

Those canvassing for votes this year can expect that many of the same issues will be raised again.

THE LEADING CANDIDATES: All three sitting deputies plus Áine Brady (FF), Michael Fitzpatrick (FF), Darren Scully (FG), Senator Kate Walsh (PD), Shane Fitzgerald (GP)

THE CAMPAIGN: Charlie McCreevy's name was on the Kildare, and later Kildare North, ballot paper for twenty-five years. This time it will be absent and much of the political speculation in the county centres on which of Fianna Fáil's two candidates will replace him. Will it be the woman who lost the by-election, Áine Brady? Or will it be Charlie McCreevy's former right hand man, Michael Fitzpatrick? It is, of course, possible that both could win.

After all, the party took 43 per cent of the vote here in 2002. But the vast bulk of that vote went, as always, to McCreevy and a significant element of it was likely to be personal rather party-political.

There has been no shortage of in-fighting in Kildare North Fianna Fáil in recent years. Local observers say there are still two distinct factions – the party HQ wing and the McCreevy wing.

Áine Brady is steeped in Fianna Fáil. Her father, Michael F Kitt, was a TD. Her husband, Gerry Brady, was a TD. Her brother, Tom Kitt, is the government chief whip and a TD for Dublin South. Another brother, Micheál P Kitt, is a member of the Seanad and a former TD for Galway East. All three siblings will be contesting this year's election. Both Brady and others within Fianna Fáil argue that if the party had run a longer by-election campaign she would have won.

Michael Fitzpatrick is a councillor for the Clane electoral area of Kildare County Council. A former Garda, he worked as Charlie McCreevy's constituency organiser for many years.

Fine Gael will also have two candidates. Maynooth-based Bernard Durkan was only 200 votes away from losing his seat in 2002. But unlike many on the Fine Gael front bench he held on. The party's second candidate is Darren Scully. He was another by-election contender and performed creditably enough, getting around 18 per cent of the vote. Scully has one big factor in his favour — he's the only candidate who lives in the county town of Naas.

Emmet Stagg has been a member of the Dáil since 1987. The Labour vote increased slightly at the last election and it would be a big surprise if he failed to be elected on this occasion.

The by-election victor, Catherine Murphy, will also be in the race again. The first women ever to represent Kildare in the Dáil, she was originally a member of the Workers Party/Democratic Left. She joined Labour when the two parties merged, but ran as an Independent in the 2004 local elections. She is based in Leixlip as is the bulk of her vote. Indeed, it was the massive vote she received from the town that secured her win in the by-election.

There will also be another Leixlip-based candidate on the ballot paper. Shane Fitzgerald, a town councillor who runs a florist and landscape gardening business, will represent the Green Party. The Greens got only 6 per cent of the Kildare North vote five years ago and he must be considered an outsider. But, again, if a significant swing towards the party emerged he could be in with a slight chance.

OUR PREDICTION: It's hard to see Emmett Stagg losing out. It would also be something of an upset if Catherine Murphy were to be ousted so soon after her by-election victory. Fine Gael will also take a seat, although it could be hard to separate Durkan and Scully. Fianna Fáil must also take a seat. Again it's hard to choose, but we'll give the nod to Aine Brady.

That would mean Kildare North, with one extra seat, would go:

1 FF, 1 FG, 1 Lab, 1 Ind – an Independent gain over the last election.

KILDARE SOUTH – THREE SEATS

SITTING DEPUTIES: Sean Power (FF), Sean Ó Fearghail (FF), Jack Wall (Lab)

THE CONSTITUENCY: Yet another disaster for Fine Gael in 2002 when the party's vote slumped by 9 per cent and former leader, Alan Dukes, lost his seat to Fianna Fáil's Sean Ó Fearghail.

Kildare South has also witnessed a population boom over the past decade. According to the preliminary census figures, the number of people living in the constituency grew by almost 18 per cent between 2002 and 2006. The effects of this surge are particularly visible around towns such as Newbridge and Athy. The other big population centres are Kildare town and Monasterevin.

Kildare South loses some of its territory in the boundary revision.

LEADING CANDIDATES: The three sitting deputies will be running again. Also on the ballot paper will be Alan Gillis (FG), Richard Daly (FG), Senator John Dardis (PD), JJ Power (GP), Threasa Bennitt (SF)

THE CAMPAIGN: Apart from the Fine Gael capitualtion, the last election campaign in Kildare South was notable for the fact that two brothers ran for two different parties. They will do so again this time. Sean Power, who is the Minister for State at the Department of Health, topped the poll for Fianna Fáil on the last occasion. His brother JJ is the Green party candidate. He took just 3.5 per cent of the vote in 2002. Their father, Paddy, was a Fianna Fáil TD for Kildare from 1969-89.

Not only did the Fianna Fáil vote increase considerably at the last election, the two candidates also managed to split that vote right down the middle. Power was just 400 votes ahead of his running mate, Sean Ó Fearghail. Ó Fearghail is a perfect example of 'if at first you don't succeed...'. It took him five general elections to make a breakthrough and he had also run unsuccessfully for the Seanad.

Alan Dukes won't be attempting to regain his seat, but the Fine Gael ticket certainly isn't short of experience. Former MEP Alan Gillis was added to the party slate after Athy-based councillor, Richard Daly, was chosen at a selection convention. This was one of several constituencies where it had been speculated that Mairead McGuinness might run, but the MEP eventually chose her native Louth.

Jack Wall will be attempting to secure a third term in the Dáil. His vote slipped slightly on the last occasion and in the end he was only a couple of hundred votes ahead of Alan Dukes. John Dardis, who is from Newbridge, will be running in his fourth General Election for the Progressive Democrats. He has always polled respectably, but has never come that close to being elected.

OUR PREDICTION: The big question, then, is whether Fine Gael can win back the seat it lost in 2002. It's certainly on the target list. But the feeling in Kildare is that this is one place where they could fall just short. The Alan Gillis vote, in particular, is hard to gauge as he hasn't been on a ballot paper since the European elections in 1999 when he lost his Brussels seat. He certainly should help shore up the Fine Gael vote in the rural parts of the constituency and is generally seen as the stronger of the two Fine Gaelers.

Jack Wall of Labour is expected to be returned.

There are differing views as to the strength of the two Fianna Fáil men with some arguing that Power might actually be more vulnerable than Ó Fearghaíl.

Fine Gael will undoubtedly do better than in 2002 when their second candidate got just 800 votes here but, on balance, we're going for no change.

LAOIS/OFFALY – FIVE SEATS

OUTGOING DEPUTIES: Brian Cowen (FF), John Moloney (FF), Sean Fleming (FF), Olwyn Enright (FG), Tom Parlon (PD).

THE CONSTITUENCY: There are no boundary changes. Laois/Offaly includes big urban centres like Tullamore and Port Laoise. It's the constituency of Finance Minister Brian Cowen and was represented for more than forty years by Oliver J Flanagan of Fine Gael.

THE LEADING CANDIDATES: The five outgoing deputies plus John Foley (FF), Charles Flanagan (FG), Mollie Buckley (FG), Jim O'Brien (Lab), David Whelan (Lab), Brian Stanley (SF), John Bracken (Ind).

THE CAMPAIGN: Laois/Offaly will be the setting of one of the most intriguing re-matches of the election with the PD's Tom Parlon going head-to-head with Charlie Flanagan of Fine Gael. In 2002 Parlon sensationally took the Flanagan seat, held continuously by Charlie Flanagan, and before him his father Oliver, for almost sixty years. Flanagan has had five years to lick his wounds. In this instance you can forget any suggestion that politics is merely business, this is personal.

On the Fine Gael ticket with Flanagan is sitting deputy, education spokesperson, Olwyn Enright, from Birr and Councillor Mollie Buckley from Tullamore. She was a candidate in the 1992 general election for Fine Gael but then spent a considerable period in local politics as an independent, before re-joining the party. It was just the Flanagan/Enright pairing in 2002, but the belief in Fine Gael now is that leaving the Tullamore area without a candidate was a mistake, which the party has now rectified by running Mollie Buckley.

Tullamore is of course the home base of Brian Cowen and recent elections have seen Cowen, and his fellow Fianna Fáil deputies, John Moloney and Sean Fleming, provide a master class in vote management. Last time they got more than 50 per cent of the votes. This time Moloney and Fleming, both Laois based, will be particularly wary of the threat from Flanagan, who is from Port Laoise.

Pat Gallagher won a seat for Labour here in 1992 and this time they've got two candidates. Jim O'Brien is from Laois and David Whelan is from Offaly. Few expect Labour to win a seat but their transfers could be vital in the shake-up for the last seat.

OUR PREDICTION: Fianna Fáil is certain to win two seats here and Fine Gael one, leaving Fianna Fáil, Fine Gael and Tom Parlon battling for the remaining two.

The PD's did poorly at the local elections here and Parlon has to be the outgoing deputy most at risk. The slick Fianna Fáil machine will probably hold their three seats but if enough of the Fine Gael voters, in Laois in particular, who defected to the PD's last time, return to Flanagan, then Tom Parlon could be the loser.

OUR PREDICATION: 3 FF and 2 FG. (Fine Gael gain from the Progressive Democrats).

LIMERICK EAST – FIVE SEATS

OUTGOING DEPUTIES: Willie O'Dea (FF), Peter Power (FF), Michael Noonan (FG), Jan O'Sullivan (Lab), Tim O'Malley (PD).

THE CONSTITUENCY: This five-seat constituency is centred on Limerick city and stretches from the outer western suburbs to the border with Tipperary to the east. It's known as 'the cradle of the PDs', having been represented for many years by Des O'Malley. The Progressive Democrats once held two seats here.

THE LEADING CANDIDATES: The outgoing deputies plus Noreen Ryan (FF), Kieran O'Donnell (FG), Trish Forde-Brennan (GP), Maurice Quinlivan (SF).

THE CAMPAIGN: The big question here is whether Tim O'Malley of the PDs can stave off the efforts of Kieran O'Donnell of Fine Gael to unseat him.

Fianna Fáil, with Willie O'Dea the third highest vote getter in the country, are certainties for two seat.

Five years ago, on a bad day nationally, Fine Gael pushed up their 1997 vote by one point. The fact that the then party leader, Michael Noonan, was also a local deputy wasn't enough to get that second seat, but his running mate, Mary Jackman, missed out by just 305 votes.

Labour will be hoping to improve on their 1997 performance. Then their vote was down by seven points.

The PDs too didn't exactly cover themselves in glory. Tim O'Malley, who took over from his cousin Des, managed less than 10 per cent of the vote, and like Jan O'Sullivan had to wait until the eleventh count before being elected.

Prior to the emergence of the Progressive Democrats Fine Gael used to have two seats here. Kieran O'Donnell the Fine Gael candidate is a nephew of long-serving TD and MEP Tom O'Donnell. We've got the prospect of a fascinating battle between two of the sons of Limerick's most prominent political families.

OUR PREDICTION: Fianna Fáil will win two seats and Michael Noonan will again ensure that Fine Gael has at least one. Traditionally there has been a Labour seat here and that shouldn't change.

There's been a steady decline in PD support in recent elections. The party hasn't a single seat on the city council. The O'Malley name has to count for something in any election in Limerick, and promises of further tax cuts, increased pensions and reduced stamp duty will also help the O'Malley campaign. But if the tide goes out for the PDs nationally at this election Limerick East could end up without an O'Malley in the Dáil for the first time since 1954. 2 FF, 2 FG, 1 Lab (Fine Gael gain from PD).

LIMERICK WEST – THREE SEATS

OUTGOING DEPUTIES: John Cregan (FF), Michael Collins (FF), Dan Neville (FG). Michael Collins is retiring.

THE CONSTITUENCY: Limerick West stretches from the outer western suburbs of Limerick city to the Kerry border. Rathkeale and Newcastle West are two of the principal population centres in this largely rural constituency; part of Limerick East in Bruff and Knockrainey moves to Limerick West. The Collins family has dominated Fianna Fáil politics here for almost sixty years.

THE LEADING CANDIDATES: The outgoing deputies, except for Michael Collins who is retiring, plus Niall Collins (FF), Michael Finucane (FG), Michael Brennan (PD).

THE CAMPAIGN: Limerick West is a Fianna Fáil stronghold. They won over 53 per cent of the vote in 2002, and if they approach anything like that in this election, they'll romp home again with two seats.

John Cregan, who got the fourth highest vote in the country last time, is again running, joined this time by the latest political product of the Collins family, Niall, a nephew of sitting deputy Michael and former deputy and minister, Gerry.

Fine Gael caused an upset here in 1997, when Dan Neville and Michael Finucane took two of the three seats. This was a consequence of internal Fianna Fáil fighting, rather than any great Fine Gael strategy. Two former Fianna Fáil members ran as independents, split the vote, and allowed Fine Gael to capitalise. But, harmony within Fianna Fáil, and the electoral status quo, was restored in 2002.

The PDs won a seat here in 1987. The memory of that victory, by John McCoy, may be fading but former Fianna Fáil senator,

Michael Brennan, hopes to revive that party's fortunes. He's expected to poll respectably and his transfers could be decisive, in particular as far as Fine Gael are concerned. In the last election the Fine Gael candidates, Finucane and Neville, were neck and neck all the way, until, after a recount, Neville made it, by one vote!

OUR PREDICTION: Fine Gael hold out faint hopes of two seats, but a change is unlikely. 2 FF, 1FG.

LONGFORD/WESTMEATH – FOUR SEATS

OUTGOING DEPUTIES: Donie Cassidy (FF), Peter Kelly (FF), Willie Penrose (Lab), Paul McGrath (FG), Mae Sexton (PD).

THE CONSTITUENCY: This is a new four-seat constituency. It now combines Longford, which previously was part of the four-seat Longford-Roscommon constituency, with the three-seat Westmeath constituency. Part of the old Westmeath constituency, in the Castlepollard area now transfers to Meath West, with the loss to Longford-Westmeath of almost six thousand votes.

THE LEADING CANDIDATES: Paul McGrath of Fine Gael is not contesting the election, leaving the other four outgoing deputies plus Senator Mary O'Rourke (FF), Senator James Bannon (FG), Nicky McFadden (FG), Peter Burke (FG) and Paul Hogan (SF).

THE CAMPAIGN: There is a real possibility that after the election three of the current deputies will not be in the next Dáil. Paul McGrath of Fine Gael is retiring, and both Donie Cassidy and Mae Sexton have mountains to climb if they are to be re-elected.

Geography and county loyalties will play crucial parts in deciding who the winners and losers will be. Mary O'Rourke was the surprise casualty in Westmeath in 2002. Athlone was left without a local deputy. The expectation is that this will be righted in the coming election with the battle for the 'Athlone seat' between the former minister, Mary O'Rourke, and Fine Gael's Nicky McFadden. Donie Cassidy has to be the unluckiest of the Westmeath-based candidates. A large slice of his Castlepollard stronghold now moves to the new Meath West constituency, and along with it go, according to Cassidy, some two thousand voters who normally would vote for him.

At the Longford end of the constituency Peter Kelly, who inherited the old Albert Reynolds seat, is the only Fianna Fáil candidate from the county and must be odds on to be returned. Mae Sexton of the Progressive Democrats, also Longford-based, will very likely be a victim of the recent constituency carve-up. She was elected in 2002 in Longford-Roscommon courtesy of a large slice of good fortune. Transfers from the independent 'Roscommon Hospital' candidate Una Quinn and Fine Gael's Louis Belton helped edge her ahead of Dr Greg Kelly of Fianna Fáil to win a seat that few predicted.

Senator James Bannon of Fine Gael is strategically very well placed. He lives in County Longford, but is right beside the Westmeath border. Willie Penrose was a poll-topper here last time with more than a quota. It would be one of the upsets of the election, nationally, if he didn't make it.

OUR PREDICTION: Longford will return at least one deputy and Peter Kelly must be the favourite by a mile. McFadden and Bannon will most probably battle it out for the one guaranteed Fine Gael seat. They could win two, but that would be a major surprise. Penrose will very likely top the poll once again. Finally we could be left with a do or die battle for a second Fianna Fáil seat between O'Rourke and Cassidy. Local polls, speculation and demography would seem to favour O'Rourke. If Cassidy is to win the seat he has to pray that O'Rourke is behind her fellow Athlone woman Nicky McFadden at the first count and that he benefits most from the transfers of other non-Athlone based candidates.

OUR PREDICATION: 2 FF, 1 Lab and 1 FG. (PD loss due to constituency change).

LOUTH – FOUR SEATS

SITTING DEPUTIES: Dermot Ahern (FF), Seamus Kirk (FF), Fergus O'Dowd (FG), Arthur Morgan (SF).

THE CONSTITUENCY: Louth might provide one of the most exciting battles in this election. Fine Gael are adamant that the arrival of Mairead McGuinness means they will take two seats here. Fianna Fáil are equally insistent that they won't.

Louth's population has risen by 9 per cent since 2002. The south of the county, in particular, has witnessed a building boom. However, some of the new houses on the outskirts of Drogheda are actually just over the boundary in the Meath East constituency.

Considering Louth's tiny size, there is no more polarised county. Drogheda people tend to vote Drogheda and Dundalk people vote Dundalk.

Health issues – in particular a string of controversies involving Our Lady of Lourdes Hospital in Drogheda – are likely to feature prominently in the campaign.

THE LEADING CANDIDATES: The four sitting deputies plus Frank Maher (FF), Jim D'Arcy (FG), Mairead McGuinness (FG), Gerald Nash (Lab), Mark Dearey (GP), Peter Short (WP), Luke Martin (Parental Equality).

THE CAMPAIGN: The fundamental question in Louth is this: can Mairead McGuinness win a seat? And if she does who will lose out? The former TV presenter got a phenomenal vote in the last

European Elections and could have run in several Dáil constituencies. In the end, she opted for her native Louth.

There can be little doubt but that the two candidates originally selected by Fine Gael – Fergus O'Dowd and Jim D'Arcy – were put out by her arrival. However, O'Dowd is in a strong position in the south of the county. Drogheda almost always elects a TD; for years that person was Labour's Michael Bell. O'Dowd has also been one of Fine Gael's better performers over the past couple of years; even his opponents acknowledge that he has done huge work in highlighting the grim conditions in some of the country's nursing homes.

The Fianna Fáil ticket is the same as in 2002. The Minister for Foreign Affairs, Dermot Ahern, is joined by backbencher Seamus Kirk and Drogheda-based councillor, Frank Maher. Ahern got more than a quota last time out and has the safest seat in the constituency.

Arthur Morgan made the breakthrough here in 2002 when he almost doubled the Sinn Féin vote. He's not a certainty for re-election, but he's probably secure enough.

Mark Dearey of the Greens and Gerald Nash of Labour can both expect to do reasonably well. Indeed, in a less competitive environment Dearey could be in contention for a seat. But the candidacy of McGuinness appears to have put paid to his chances.

OUR PREDICTION: Expect every cliché in the election handbook to be used on count day: battle royal, dogfight, photo-finish – this could be all of those and more.

The logic says that Fianna Fáil shouldn't lose their second seat here. The party got 44 per cent of the Louth vote in 2002. Fine Gael got less than half that. But an opinion poll for the Drogheda Independent suggested that Mairead McGuinness could take a seat without Fergus O'Dowd losing his. Seamus Kirk was the most likely casualty. Fine Gael says this mirrors their own poll findings. Fianna Fáil says Dublin-based pundits are underestimating the trojan constituency work done by Kirk.

It could all come down to how the two parties manage their respective votes and to the transfers of Dearey and Nash.

OUR PREDICATION: We're going for a Fine Gael gain but won't be surprised if Kirk holds on. 1 FF, 2FG, 1SF.

MAYO – FIVE SEATS

OUTGOING DEPUTIES: John Carty (FF), Enda Kenny (FG), Michael Ring (FG), Dr Jerry Cowley (Ind), Beverley Flynn (Ind).

THE CONSTITUENCY: The five-seat Mayo constituency encompasses the county and was created by joining the two three-seat constituencies of Mayo East and Mayo West.

THE LEADING CANDIDATES: All five outgoing deputies plus Dara Calleary (FF), Frank Chambers (FF), Michelle Mulherin (FG), John O'Mahony (FG), Gerry Murray (SF).

THE CAMPAIGN: If Fine Gael can't gain a seat in the party leader's constituency, then it will surely find it difficult to make significant gains elsewhere. Beverley Flynn once of Fianna Fáil, whose father Padraig was first elected here in 1977, could well be fighting for her political life come the election. If Fianna Fáil were to come back with two of the five seats it would be a cause for some celebration. The party is still reeling from the fallout from the Flynn affair and it's no secret that morale in Mayo isn't exactly sky high. Five years ago the stranglehold the two main parties had was broken with the surprise election of Dr Jerry Cowley, campaigning essentially on the need for improvements in the health services. Since then, of course, the controversy in the Rossport area regarding the Shell off-shore gas developments is another powerful and emotive issue that could be a vital campaign issue here.

OUR PREDICTION: The possibilities that Mayo throws up are fascinating. Can it return three Fine Gael deputies, as it did in 1997? How will the expulsion of Beverley Flynn affect the Fianna Fáil party and can she hold her seat as an independent? Can Dr Jerry Cowley repeat or improve on his 2002 showing? And how will Gerry Murray of Sinn Féin fair? He was first elected as a Fianna Fáil councillor and is a formidable vote-getter who has helped build up his party's organisation in the constituency. The Rossport controversy has provided Sinn Féin with an important local issue. He could well be the dark horse.

From the Fianna Fáil perspective, can regional loyalties help Dara Calleary from Ballina make it? His father Sean was a TD in Mayo East for many years. Ballina doesn't currently have a deputy but if Calleary were to take a seat here it could be at the incumbent, John Carthy's, expense.

If Fine Gael is to win three of the five seats here, the selection of John O'Mahony, the current manager of the county's Gaelic football team, who is based in the old Mayo East part of the constituency, could prove to be an inspired decision.

OUR PREDICTION: 3 FG, 1 FF, 1 Ind

MEATH EAST – THREE SEATS

OUTGOING DEPUTIES: Mary Wallace (FF), Shane McEntee (FG).

THE CONSTITUENCY: A sharp rise in population means that the old five-seat constituency of Meath has been split in two. In its place are two new three-seaters: Meath East and Meath West.

That growth has continued apace since the boundary review, and Meath East will still have one of the highest population numbers per TD in the country.

Meath East includes areas such as Bettystown, Dunshaughlin, Ashbourne and Dunboyne. This is commuter-country and, not surprisingly, many of the issues here are connected to the growth of the past decade. A look at the local papers any week will yield stories about issues such as planning and traffic congestion. A local controversy that attracted national headlines was the case of the primary school in Laytown which was so chronically overcrowded that some children could only attend in the afternoon. A new building has since been promised.

It's also likely that many of those voting in Meath East will be voting for the first time in this particular constituency. Adding to the unpredictability, local political watchers say, is the fact that Meath voted electronically in 2002. This means there were no tallies.

THE LEADING CANDIDATES: Wallace and McEntee plus Thomas Byrne (FF), Regina Doherty (FG), Dominic Hannigan (Lab), Brian Fitzgerald (Ind), Sirena Campbell (PD), Joanne Finnegan (SF), Sean Ó Buachalla (GP).

THE CAMPAIGN: Mary Wallace, who is based in Ratoath, was a Junior Minister in the 1997-2002 coalition but was dropped after the last election. She was controversially reinstated in early 2006. At the time, some within Fianna Fáil asked whether there were others more deserving of the half car. Some political commentators argued that the decision was motivated largely by the desire to try and shore up the Fianna Fáil vote in the new constituency.

Whatever your opinion, she is seen as a safe-bet for re-election. Shane McEntee, who took a seat in the by-election following John

Bruton's departure for Washington is also likely to be returned.

The other candidate most widely tipped for electoral success is Dominic Hannigan of the Labour Party. Indeed, if you ask many political observers to name potential gains for Labour across the country, his could well be the first name you hear. Initially elected to Meath County Council as an Independent in 2004, Dominic Hannigan switched to the Labour Party shortly afterwards. He was the party's candidate in the March 2005 Meath by-election when he secured just over 11 per cent of the vote, a considerable improvement on the 4 per cent Labour received in 2002.

It should be said, however, that the former Labour TD, Brian Fitzgerald, didn't stand in that by-election. He did run in 2002 and will be on the ballot paper again this time. A county councillor for the Dunshaughlin electoral area, he left the party in protest at the merger with Democratic Left. His one term as a TD was from 1992-97. While he will undoubtedly take votes from Dominic Hannigan, his vote has declined since the heady days of the 'Spring Tide'.

This is one of those constituencies, on the fringes of Dublin, where if the Green Party had a more established candidate they could probably be expected to do fairly well. But Sean Ó Buachalla could be too late an entrant to the field to have any huge impact.

OUR PREDICTION: There have been local reports suggesting that Thomas Byrne's campaign has been going well and that he could be in with a serious shout for the third seat. That may well be the case, but you'll still find a greater number of observers giving Dominic Hannigan the nod.

That would mean the breakdown here would be one Fianna Fail, one Fine Gael and one Labour, the extra seat in Meath bringing a gain for the alternative coalition.

MEATH WEST – THREE SEATS

OUTGOING DEPUTIES: Noel Dempsey (FF), Johnny Brady (FF), Damien English (FG).

THE CONSTITUENCY: This new three-seater consists, as the name implies, of the western part of County Meath. In the boundary revision, a small part of County Westmeath was also included.

Agriculture is still important in parts of this constituency, but tellingly, a place once synonymous with big farmers is now equally synonymous with harassed commuters. In many of the new housing estates on the outskirts of Navan, the vast majority of residents have to undertake the daily drive to and from Dublin. There is no rail-link between Navan and the capital. One has been pledged on several occasions, but is not due to be completed until 2015. A local lobby-group has been doing its best to ensure that this is an election issue.

Another local transport controversy centres on the route of the M3 motorway through the Tara-Skryne Valley. While the plans have generated a huge amount of debate at a national level, locals say this is unlikely to be a big election issue. What is a big political issue in the Navan area, however, is the proposed development of the Fair Green although, again, it's not clear whether the row will have any significant impact on how people vote.

THE LEADING CANDIDATES: The sitting deputies plus Graham Geraghty (FG), Peter Higgins (FG), Joe Reilly (SF), Brian Collins (Lab), Brian Flanagan (GP).

THE CAMPAIGN: Meath West is one of several constituencies where men better known for their ability on the sports field than on the hustings will be attempting to make it to the Dáil.

In this case the contender is Fine Gael representative, and county footballer, Graham Geraghty who described the party selection convention as 'ten times more nerve-racking than an All-Ireland final'. He is one of three Fine Gael candidates and, in the view of some, that's one candidate too many.

Fianna Fáil have just two candidates and both are sitting TDs – the Minister for Communications, Marine and Natural Resources, Noel Dempsey who is from Trim and backbencher, Johnny Brady, who is from Kells in the northern end of the constituency. A number of areas where he has polled strongly in the past will actually be in the Meath East constituency this time, and it is generally believed that he would have been in a more comfortable position had the county been split north-south.

Another of the contenders here would rather the constituency hadn't been split at all. The Sinn Féin candidate, Joe Reilly, who's a Navan-based councillor, polled strongly in the 2002 election. He got almost 10 per cent of the first-preference vote, but fell short of getting elected. Had the constituency remained a five-seater he would have been strongly tipped for success on this occasion. However, the down-sizing to a three-seater is reckoned to have put paid to his chances.

There is no candidate based over the county-line in Westmeath and the voters there can expect to find themselves fought over by several of the hopefuls. Peter Higgins of Fine Gael might be better-placed than most as he is originally from Castlepollard. Indeed, his uncle was a member of Westmeath County Council albeit for Fianna Fáil!

OUR PREDICTION: What is clear, according to political followers in Meath West, is that Noel Dempsey will be elected to the Dáil. He topped the poll, with more than a quota, in Meath at the last election. Fine Gael can also be expected to take a seat and

Damien English must be the front-runner, having worked hard to secure his position since his surprise election in 2002.

But what about number three? Fine Gael are adamant that they can take it. As, indeed, is Sinn Féin's Joe Reilly. The bookies, however, don't tend to get these things too wrong and one leading chain seems so certain that Johnny Brady will be re-elected that it is offering no price on him (this is also the case for Dempsey and English).

It mightn't be the most exciting prediction, then, but it seems the money is the return of the three sitting TDs: 2 Fianna Fáil, 1 Fine Gael.

ROSCOMMON/SOUTH LEITRIM – THREE SEATS

SITTING DEPUTIES: John Ellis (FF), Michael Finneran (FF), Denis Naughton (FG).

THE CONSTITUENCY: This is a new constituency. Roscommon has been decoupled from Longford and instead is paired with the southern part of county Leitrim. Leitrim's division (the northern end remains with Sligo) caused ructions locally with complaints that the county could end up with no representative in the Dáil.

After decades of decline, South Leitrim has seen a steady rise in its population in recent years. Carrick-on-Shannon, in particular, has experienced a building boom. Bank of America, formerly MBNA, has created a considerable number of jobs.

For many years, the big political issue in Roscommon was the future of the county hospital. Back in 1989, Tom Foxe was elected as an Independent on a 'save the hospital' platform. He also took a seat in 1992. It had appeared that this issue was in abeyance. But it has re-emerged with some force. At a public meeting last year, the

Roscommon Fianna Fáil TD, Michael Finneran, said he would not stand for the party in the General Election if proposals to withdraw in-patient surgery facilities at the hospital were accepted by the Government. He says he has since received reassurances from the cabinet.

THE LEADING CANDIDATES: The three sitting TDs plus Senator Frank Feighan (FG), Hugh Baxter (Lab), Martin Kenny (SF), Garreth McDaid (GP), John Kelly (Ind).

THE CAMPAIGN: Barring something very strange happening, there will be at last one Fianna Fáil seat in this constituency and at least one for Fine Gael. There are a number of reasons why this could be an intriguing contest.

Denis Naughton (FG) is an outgoing TD for Longford/Roscommon and looks pretty safe. His running mate, Frank Feighan, is from Boyle in North Roscommon.

Michael Finneran entered Leinster House as a member of the Seanad in 1989, but made it to the Dáil for the first time in 2002.

John Ellis is an outgoing Fianna Fáil TD for Sligo/Leitrim. He is one of three Leitrim-based candidates (the other two are Martin Kenny of Sinn Féin and Garreth McDaid of the Greens). Ellis can probably expect a very strong vote from his own county but on the last occasion he was elected with the help of transfers from his Sligo-based colleagues. It is thought he might find it difficult to attract as many Roscommon transfers.

There had been persistent speculation that Fianna Fáil would add a third candidate and that this would be Rachel Doherty, daughter of the late Sean Doherty. She is a county councillor in the Boyle area and could have had an impact of Frank Feighan's vote.

Garreth McDaid has an interesting political background. A first time candidate, his father is the former Fianna Fáil Minister – and Donegal North East candidate – Dr Jim McDaid. The Greens got less than 1 per cent of the vote in the Longford/Roscommon constituency last time out.

A question-mark still hangs over the intentions of the Roscommon Hospital Action Committee. There is a strong chance that they will back an Independent candidate, but they have yet to produce a name. In 2002 their candidate, Una Quinn, got more than 7 per cent of the vote. Her elimination elected Denis Naughton. The view on the ground is that if the Committee does endorse a candidate considerable damage could be done to Michael Finneran's vote.

OUR PREDICTION: This is a constituency where Fine Gael could pick up a seat. Having said that it's hard to see either Ellis or Finneran, who are both experienced campaigners, going without a fight. We're cautiously predicting a gain for Fine Gael, with the decision of the Roscommon Hospital Action Committee having a bearing on the final result.

SLIGO/NORTH LEITRIM – THREE SEATS

SITTING DEPUTIES: Dr Jimmy Devins (FF), John Perry (FG), Marian Harkin (Ind). All three are outgoing TDs for the old Sligo/Leitrim constituency. Marian Harkin is also an MEP and is opting to stay in Brussels.

THE CONSTITUENCY: This is another new constituency created following the recommendations of the Constituency Commission. Only the northern part of County Leitrim remains paired with Sligo and the number of TDs will drop from four to three.

North Leitrim is predominantly rural. Its main town is Manorhamilton. The bulk of voters will be in the Sligo part of the constituency, adding fuel to the fears of people in Leitrim that it could become the only county without a TD.

The big story in this region five years ago was the election of Independent candidate, Marian Harkin. She topped the poll with more than 17 per cent of the vote. The big losers were Fine Gael and Labour whose votes were down by almost 10 per cent and almost 6 per cent respectively. Fine Gael's Gerry Reynolds lost his seat. The Fianna Fáil vote was also down slightly.

In general, the big issues here are local variations on national controversies. There are complaints from the opposition and from voters that this part of the country is still lagging behind the eastern seaboard when it comes to investment. Those complaints helped Marian Harkin secure her considerable vote on the last occasion and probably shouldn't be taken lightly. One of the health issues that has caused controversy is the delay in extending the Breastcheck programme to the northwest.

THE LEADING CANDIDATES: Jimmy Devins and John Perry plus Senator Eamon Scanlon (FF), Imelda Henry (FG), Michael Comiskey (FG), Jim McGarry (Lab), Sean McManus (SF).

THE CAMPAIGN: The other candidates will disagree, but the main question here is whether this new constituency will divide 2FF, 1FG or 2FG, 1FF. There is no doubt that John Perry will be elected; the man who brought the Mayor of New York, Michael Bloomberg, to Ballymote is widely regarded as a wily operator. Jimmy Devins of Fianna Fáil, whose base is in Sligo Town, should also be returned.

But where to from there? There was a time when Sean McManus of Sinn Féin was seen as a possible contender. He says himself that he wouldn't be running unless he thought there was a genuine chance he could take a seat. Five years ago he got 5,001 votes – that's just over ten per cent. He could benefit from the fact that Marian Harkin won't be on the ballot paper this time out. But realistically in a three-seat constituency, with a sizeable number of his former voters now in the Roscommon South-Leitrim constituency, it's hard to see him making it.

The Labour candidate, Jim McGarry, is a county councillor and former member of Fine Gael. By all accounts, there is no love lost between himself and the one-time Labour TD, Declan Bree. Again, it's hard to see McGarry in the final-shakeup.

Marian Harkin's success showed that there is scope for an Independent candidate here. A number of names, some political and some less so, have been suggested as possible independent candidates. The most likely is Margaret Gormley, an Independent county councillor based in south Sligo. She has confirmed that she is considering a bid for the Dáil but, at the time of going to print, still hadn't made a final decision. There are also strong indications that Declan Bree could run as an Independent, but at the time of writng he had not made a final decision.

A TG4 opinion poll, conducted in this constituency just before Christmas, suggested that the final seat would go to either Eamon Scanlon of Fianna Fáil, who like John Perry is from Ballymote, or Michael Comiskey from Fine Gael. Well known for his involvement with the IFA, he is the only candidate based in Leitrim.

The Fine Gael hope is that Comiskey can secure the majority of the Leitrim votes, keeping him in the race until the party's third candidate, Sligo councillor Imelda Henry is eliminated at which point her transfers will help to elect him. Fianna Fáil are relying on their vote being strong enough and well-balanced enough to ensure that both candidates are elected.

OUR PREDICTION: Fine Gael are certainly targeting this constituency. The party held their last 'think-in' in Sligo town with Enda Kenny telling the local media that two out of three was the aim. It will be a photofinish, but we'll go for: 2FF, 1 FG.

TIPPERARY NORTH – THREE SEATS

OUTGOING DEPUTIES: Michael Smith (FF), Máire Hoctor (FF), Michael Lowry (Ind).

THE CONSTITUENCY: Described as the ultimate 'bell-weather' constituency, North Tipperary has long been seen as a pretty accurate gauge of the national trend. This picture may have been changed somewhat, however, by the Michael Lowry factor. The fact that he left Fine Gael, but held on to much of the party's vote has seen them fail to win a seat here at the last two elections.

North Tipperary is a predominantly rural constituency, though there are considerably fewer people who rely on farming for their sole income. The main towns are Thurles, Nenagh and Roscrea.

The future of Nenagh General Hospital, due to be downgraded under the Hanly Report, is always an issue here. Indeed, it lead to an almighty row within Fianna Fáil during the last Dáil term with Michael Smith publicly opposing Hanly while his party colleague, Máire Hoctor, toed the government line. The then-Defence Minister was forced to apologise to a furious Bertie Ahern and was later demoted to the back-benches.

THE LEADING CANDIDATES: The three outgoing TDs plus Senator Noel Coonan (FG), Senator Kathleen O'Meara (Lab), Seamus Morris (SF), Jim Ryan (Ind).

THE CAMPAIGN: It may get up a lot of people's noses, particularly in Dublin, but Michael Lowry will win a seat here as he has done at every election since 1987. Whatever his travails with the Moriarty Tribunal, which has been conducting a lengthy investigation into the former Minister's financial relationship with businessman Denis O'Brien, he is still well regarded in North Tipp, particularly in and around Thurles.

There is a view, however, that he may not top the poll on this occasion. This could be partly because, as in 2002, another slice of his vote may return to Fine Gael. Another reason could be the candidacy of Jim Ryan. Ryan is a former Fianna Fáil councillor – his grandfather was a founder-member of the party – who fell out with some of the local party grandees. He joined the Independent ranks prior to the last local elections and secured a sizeable vote in Thurles.

Jim Ryan is unlikely to make it to Leinster House, but as well as taking Lowry votes it's believed that he could also harm the Michael Smith vote. In a long political career, Smith has failed to get elected on three occasions (although it must be said the last such time was November 1982) and is not invincible.

Nenagh-based Máire Hoctor is now seen as the more secure of the Fianna Fáil TDs and has been tipped by a number of politics-watchers to top the poll.

But there will be quite a bit of competition for the Nenagh vote. Seamie Morris of Sinn Féin, headed the poll in the last town council elections and has been building up a reasonable profile in the constituency. The party had no candidate here in 2002, and there will be a lot of interest in how he performs.

Kathleen O'Meara of Labour is also from Nenagh. This will be her third attempt to win back a seat for the party in this constituency.

The Fine Gael candidate, Noel Coonan, is from Templemore and will be fighting his second general election.

OUR PREDICTION: It will be tight but one way or another Michael Lowry and Máire Hoctor are likely to be elected. If that is the case, the third seat should come down to a three-way contest between Smith, Coonan and O'Meara. It could go to any of them.

But there is a belief that if O'Meara is the first of the three to be eliminated, her transfers will elect Coonan.

Two health warnings should be given with this assumption. The first is that Michael Smith is a doughty campaigner who has been written off before and survived. The second is that in 2002 almost 43 per cent of Kathleen O'Meara's transfers went to either Smith or Hoctor! It's reasonable to assume, though, that the transfers between Labour and Fine Gael will be tighter on this occasion. If they are, we could be looking at a Fianna Fáil loss to Fine Gael in North Tipperary.

TIPPERARY SOUTH – THREE SEATS

SITTING DEPUTIES: Noel Davern (FF), Tom Hayes (FG), Seamus Healy (Ind). Noel Davern is retiring.

THE CONSTITUENCY: All three outgoing TDs were re-elected in 2002, but Noel Davern's decision to leave the Dáil ensures that there will be at least one change here this time.

Clonmel is the largest town in this constituency, which also includes a small part of County Waterford. The other big population centres are Carrick-on-Suir, Cashel and Tipperary Town.

One of the bigger political controversies here in recent times involved Fine Gael's decision to remove the whip from a party councillor. Michael Fitzgerald fell out with the Fine Gael hierarchy after a local radio interview in which he admitted to drink-driving and expressed understanding for those living in rural areas who drove home from the pub after consuming alcohol. Afterwards he said he had received a deluge of support and was contemplating running as an Independent. At the time of writing he had not made a final decision.

THE CANDIDATES: Two of the sitting deputies, plus Senator Martin Mansergh (FF), Siobhan Ambrose (FF), Mattie McGrath (FF), Phil Prendergast (Lab), Richie Molloy (PD), Liam Browne (SF)

THE CAMPAIGN: Going into this election campaign there are several big questions in this constituency. There is no consensus on which of Fianna Fáil's hopefuls will win a seat and opinion is divided on whether Seamus Healy will be ousted by his former colleague on the Clonmel Workers and Unemployed Action Group, Phil Prendergast.

It's hard to imagine three more different candidates than those running for Fianna Fáil in Tipperary South. At a national level, by far the best known is Senator Martin Mansergh whose base is in Tipperary Town. Last time out he was Noel Davern's running mate and the Oxford-educated advisor to the Taoiseach put in a stronger performance than some pundits had anticipated; Fianna Fáil were never likely to take a second seat, but Mansergh took over 14 per cent of the vote and must be seen as a contender on this occasion.

Siobhan Ambrose is a councillor in Clonmel. She has been highly visible in recent months, causing some to claim that she is Fianna Fáil HQ's favourite. This has lead to tensions, with one Fianna Fáil councillor accusing her of 'abducting' Ministers who visited the constituency. Her family has long been associated with Noel Davern.

Mattie McGrath is a member of South Tipperary County Council for the Cahir electoral area. At the time of going to print, he was facing a number of charges, including assault, arising out of an incident in his home village of Newcastle. He has pleaded not guilty. It had been reported that he might be removed from the party ticket and Fianna Fáil say they are keeping the situation under review. His supporters, however, have warned that there could be a 'major split' if his name isn't on the ballot paper and it appears unlikely that the party will drop him.

Seamus Healy was first elected to the Dáil in a by-election in June 2000 following the death of Labour Party TD Michael Ferris. A Labour member in his youth, Healy first ran for the Dáil as an Independent candidate in 1989. As an Independent allied to Healy's Workers and Unemployed Action Group, Phil Prendergast topped the poll in Clonmel at the local elections. She subsequently joined the Labour Party. Labour's hope is that her personal support combined with their traditional vote will help them to regain a seat in South Tipp. Healy, however, remains a formidable opponent.

Tom Hayes was one of only a handful of Fine Gael candidates to top the poll on the last occasion. He's from Golden in the west of the constituency. Michael Fitzgerald, the councillor at the centre of the drink-driving row, is from the same part of the county and has also worked with Hayes on many issues. If Fitzgerald does decide to run as an Independent there is little doubt but that he would take votes from the Fine Gael TD. He topped the poll in the last local elections and, while many mightn't necessarily agree with his views on drink-driving, his comments about the increasing isolation of rural Ireland appear to have struck a chord.

OUR PREDICTION: There are two big imponderables here – will Michael Fitzgerald run for election and what will happen in the Mattie McGrath court case.

Even if Fitzgerald does declare, it is still likely that Tom Hayes will be re-elected.

Seamus Healy got double the vote of the Labour Party candidate here in 2002. It is likely to be closer this time but we reckon he will prevail.

As for Fianna Fáil, well, Mattie McGrath has been seen by many as the frontrunner. It's unclear, though, how his legal situation will affect his chances; the case is due back in court in early May. Siobhan Ambrose has a number of advantages, among them being based in Clonmel. Martin Mansergh doesn't have the same geographic advantage, but he did put in a respectable performance on the last occasion. Overall, Mattie McGrath may still be the slight favourite, but neither of his running mates can be ruled out.

1FG, 1FF, 1 Ind, – no change

WATERFORD – FOUR SEATS

OUTGOING DEPUTIES: Martin Cullen (FF), Ollie Wilkinson (FF), John Deasy (FG), Brian O'Shea (Lab).

THE CONSTITUENCY: Waterford is not known as an exciting constituency, but this election might be different.

Interestingly, though, Waterford does like to see itself as a microcosm of the country, so if there is a major swing it's likely to be replicated here. Local journalists say this view is backed up by the fact that the turnout tends to be in-line with the national figure. Geographically, there's also a bit of everything, from the industry of Waterford city to the large town of Dungarvan in the west to the mountains in the north.

The Fianna Fáil vote went up here by 10 per cent in 2002. That figure surprised a few people, principally because of the huge local campaign about the lack of radiotherapy facilities in the south east. You might recall the Taoiseach's car being pelted with daffodils when he visited the constituency.

Some of the sting has now been taken out of this issue by an arrangement whereby public cancer patients will have access to the facilities at a new private clinic just outside Waterford city. In the main, politicians can expect to be asked about local versions of national issues, such as the health service, transport and education. Another long-running local controversy is the campaign for university status for Waterford Institute of Technology.

THE LEADING CANDIDATES: The four sitting deputies plus Brendan Kenneally (FF), Jim D'Arcy (FG), Paudie Coffey (FG), David Cullinane (SF), John Halligan (WP), Brendan McCann (GP), Mary Roche (Ind).

THE CAMPAIGN: The main challenge to the current line up is likely to come from Sinn Féin's David Cullinane. The party went from having no candidate in 1997 to getting more than 6 per cent of the first preference vote in 2002. Cullinane then ran in the 2004 local and European elections. He took more than 30,000 votes in the south constituency, two-thirds of them in Waterford. He was, however, the only one of the ten candidates from Waterford. Sinn Féin certainly see him as a strong prospect. He could be seen just over Gerry Adams's shoulder on the platform at the policing Ard Fheis.

In much of the talk of a Sinn Féin gain, Brian O'Shea's seat has been named as the most vulnerable. Not surprisingly, Labour people see it differently and argue that the second Fianna Fáil seat is more likely to fall prey to any surge in David Cullinane's vote. But the most commonly expressed view now is that the Sinn Féin man will fall short on this occasion.

On the Fianna Fáil front, there have been some rumblings about Martin Cullen's vote being down, but in the constituency there is a general expectation that the party will hold on to the two seats. There is also every chance that Brendan Kenneally, who was ousted by his running mate Ollie Wilkinson in 2002, could get the nod this time.

Local observers feel that once again Fine Gael will take one seat – and that John Deasy is the overwhelming favourite. There is some disappointment, however, that he has fallen out of favour with the party leadership and that, should Enda Kenny become Taoiseach, he is unlikely to be made a Minister.

The Workers' Party influence in Waterford may have dissipated somewhat but they are still around. John Halligan topped the poll in his ward in the 2004 city council elections. But the party's vote fell substantially in the last general election and, realistically, he's unlikely to be in contention for a seat on this occasion.

Mary Roche, who's also a city councilor, was formerly a member of Fianna Fáil. It was reported that she had been approached by the Progressive Democrats. Again, there are few who see her taking a seat, but she is expected to get a reasonable first preference vote and her transfers could be influential.

OUR PREDICTION: Overall, then, the feeling is that, with the possible exception of a change in the Fianna Fáil personnel, Waterford will once again remain unchanged at 2 FF, 1 FG and 1 Lab. A dangerous thing to say!

WEXFORD – FIVE SEATS

OUTGOING DEPUTIES: John Browne (FF), Tony Dempsey (FF), Paul Kehoe (FG), Liam Twomey (FG), Brendan Howlin (Lab). Tony Dempsey (FF) is retiring.

THE CONSTITUENCY: In 2002, a string of unheralded Independents made it to the Dáil. None was a bigger surprise than Liam Twomey. The Rosslare-based general practitioner ran on a health issues platform and took almost 10 per cent of the first preference vote.

His success was bad news for Fine Gael. Following Ivan Yates's retirement to spend more time with his bookmakers' shops, the party was in disarray and ended up with just one seat. Two years later, however, Twomey pulled off another surprise. He joined Fine Gael.

That brought the overall party strength in Wexford back to where it was post the four previous elections – 2 Fianna Fail, 2 Fine Gael, 1 Labour. Liam Twomey's election apart, then, Wexford has been a pretty stable constituency over the past couple of decades. So it's easy to see why local pundits think no change is the most likely option this year.

THE LEADING CANDIDATES: Four of the five outgoing deputies plus Sean Connick (FF), Lisa McDonald (FF), Michael D'Arcy Jnr (FG), John Dwyer (SF), Colm O'Gorman (PD)

THE CAMPAIGN: The surprise candidate here is Colm O'Gorman. A total newcomer to electoral politics, he came to national prominence through his work as founder of 'One in Four', a group that works with victims of sexual violence. Prior to the announcement that he was running for the PDs, he had held talks with Labour. His father was a Fianna Fáil councillor in Wexford.

Colm O'Gorman's candidacy received huge media attention. But an MRBI/TG4 opinion poll suggested he wasn't having the same impact with voters. The poll carried out last November put him at one per cent. Even if you don't share O'Gorman's belief that he will win a seat, it is highly unlikely that come polling day his vote will be as low as this.

It should be said that the margin of error in constituency polls is quite high, and that polls taken several months in advance of an election do tend to favour incumbents, but that survey pointed to Minister at the Department of Communications, Marine and Natural Resources John Browne topping the poll with Brendan Howlin and Paul Kehoe also being elected.

Those are predictions with which few in the constituency would quarrel. What then of the other two seats? Well, unless there is a collapse in the party vote there should be a second Fianna Fáil seat, and Sean Connick seems best placed to take it.

John Dwyer of Sinn Féin got more than 8 per cent of the vote here in 2002, a figure he matched in the East constituency at the subsequent European Elections.

Wexford is definitely a target constituency for Sinn Féin, but it's thought that he will have a tougher battle than some of his colleagues elsewhere in the country. One of the main reasons for this is the fact that Sean Connick is also from New Ross. The Fianna Fáil man took a markedly higher share of the town's vote in the last local elections.

So, while Dwyer should be taken seriously, the more likely scenario, according to people in Wexford, is that the spare seat will go to Fine Gael.

Opinion locally is divided as to which of the two remaining Fine Gaelers is likely to join Paul Kehoe in the next Dáil. Some favour Michael D'Arcy Jnr because of his Gorey base. The population in the north of the county has been increasing steadily, yet the bulk of candidates are in the centre and south of the county. Though, that was also the case in 2002 and D'Arcy's father, Michael Snr, still lost his seat.

Liam Twomey accepts that joining Fine Gael will cost him the allegiance of some of his old voters. But he argues that it will also gain him some new ones. He, certainly, has a higher profile than his running mate but again, as 2002 showed, that doesn't grant immunity from defeat.

On 'The Constituency', Tom Mooney who's the editor of the county's *Echo* newspapers reckoned the Rosslare man would shade it, and we'll go with that.

OUR PREDICTION: 2 FF, 1 Lab and 2 FG.

WICKLOW – FIVE SEATS

OUTGOING DEPUTIES: Dick Roche (FF), Joe Jacob (FF), Billy Timmins (FG), Liz McManus (Lab), Mildred Fox (Ind).

THE CONSTITUENCY: Includes all of the county plus small pockets of County Carlow near Rathvilly and Hacketstown.

THE LEADING CANDIDATES: Both Mildred Fox and Joe Jacob have decided to retire from the Dáil and will not contest the next election. That leaves the three other outgoing deputies plus Nicky Kelly (LAB), Deirdre de Burca (GP), Joe Behan (FF), Pat Fitzgerald (FF), Andrew Doyle (FG), Pat Doran (IND).

THE CAMPAIGN: It is odds on that either Labour or the Greens will pick up a seat here. Mildred Fox, who represented Wicklow since 1995 as an Independent, has decided to bow out of active politics. Her organisation has decided not to contest the election, leaving the door open for either party.

After a week of recounts in 2002 Fox held her seat, by just nineteen votes from Labour's Nicky Kelly who therefore has a strong chance of winning this time.

The decision of the Arklow based Joe Jacob to step down means that Wicklow will elect a second new TD, most probably either Councillor Joe Behan or Pat Fitzgerald, a councillor on the Arklow local authority, both from Fianna Fáil.

Billy Timmins of Fine Gael held his seat in 2002, but was returned with the lowest Fine Gael vote in Wicklow since 1951. This time he faces strong internal competition from his running mate, Councillor Andrew Doyle, a big poll topper in Wicklow town in the last local election.

Another candidate hotly tipped to be in the final shake up for the Fox seat is the Green Party candidate, Bray based councillor Deirdre de Burca.

Where that fifth seat goes could well be decided by a combination of regional loyalties and which candidate benefits most from the division of the Mildred Fox vote.

Fianna Fáil should take two seats and Labour's Liz McManus should also make it. There is a definite Fine Gael seat here, probably Billy Timmins, but no one is writing off Andrew Doyle.

Councillor Pat Doran, running as an independent after 35 years membership of Fianna Fáil, is based in the south of the county and he is bound to erode the vote of the Arklow based Fianna Fáil candidate, Pat Fitzgerald, enhancing the chances of his running mate Joe Behan joining environment minister Dick Roche in Leinster House. If this were to pass there would be three Bray based deputies, making it extremely difficult for the Greens' de Burca to make the breakthrough. In that event, Kelly would be the favourite to take that fifth seat.

OUR PREDICTION: 2 FF, 2 Lab and 1 FG.

Rachael English is the presenter of 'The Constituency', a weekly politics programme on RTÉ Radio 1. She has worked as a reporter and presenter on most of RTÉ radio's current affairs programmes including 'Morning Ireland' and the 'News at One'. She has presented General, European and Local Election results programmes. After six years as presenter of the drivetime radio programme, 'Five–Seven Live', she decided to leave last year. A communications graduate of Dublin City University, Rachael began her career with Clare FM radio in Ennis.

Nick Coffey worked in RTÉ current affairs and news for more than thirty years, on programmes such as 'Seven

Days', 'Today Tonight' and 'The Week in Politics'. He retired in October 2002. For the past year he has contributed a weekly constituency analysis in the run up to the general election on radio's 'Five–Seven Live'and latterly 'Drivetime'.